THE ART OF THE DATE

RORI SASSOON

DR. ERROL GLUCK

AN A & G PRESS BOOK, April 2019

The Art of the Date
Copyright © 2019 by Rori Sassoon and Dr. Errol Gluck
All Rights Reserved

ISBN: 0578462222
eBook ISBN: 978-0578462226

A & G Press
New York
aandgpress.com
Published in the United States of America

Dedication

Love is the most potent force of healing, of pleasure, and of creating. This book is dedicated to actualizing your ability to find that true love that will change your life unlike anything that you have ever experienced. We will celebrate with you every step of the way. This book is for you and everyone who you believe needs to find and keep true love.

Introduction

Ever wanted to date like a billionaire?

The Art of the Date shares relationship secrets from Platinum Poire, New York's most selective matchmaking agency. We match only the most elite couples: power players, movers and shakers, and super eligible CEOs. With a success rate that is second to none, we know how to choose a relationship that is built to last—and can make you richer, too!

We use our decades of combined knowledge to coach New York City's most desirable executives. Now, we're giving you an exclusive look at *how* we create relationships at the C-Suite level. Whether you want to marry a millionaire or find a relationship that will last a lifetime, we know how to get you there. Finally, you have a solution to years of bad dates and relationships that go nowhere. With our method, you can commit without compromise and get the kind of relationship you desire and deserve.

We met several years ago, when Rori was looking to overcome of her fear of highway driving. She searched for "Manhattan's best hypnotist" and found Dr. Gluck. Within a few sessions, her fears were lifted, and she was inspired by the power of profiling to help her become her best self. Dr.

Gluck saw Rori's passion for style and her incredible intuition, work ethic, and sassy-classy attitude. He'd had the idea of a matchmaking agency for years, but until he met Rori he wasn't sure the dream was a possibility. He knew that she was a perfect fit.

We went out for dinner, talked business, and the rest is history. You could say it was a match made in Manhattan.

Soon, we decided to combine our highly specialized skills to create a matchmaking agency for New York's one percent. Every year, we help hundreds of carefully selected, high profile clients find their soulmates and make meaningful connections. Now, that doesn't mean we always agree! But we always find a solution, and more importantly, we believe that love *always* finds a way.

You've seen Rori on *The Real Housewives of New York*. She's a stylist and relationship expert who offers the feminine perspective on love. She knows how important reputation is for your relationship: to command respect, be respectable. She'll also tell you what's up with guys: how to tell when you're being played, and how to attract your Mister Perfect.

Dr. Gluck, with a degree that integrates psychology, anthropology, and theology, plus decades of experience in Executive Life Coaching, forensic profiling, and the practice of neuroplasticity, speaks up for men.

From the first kiss to the first wedding anniversary, healthy marriages all use the same ingredients. Billionaires and bus drivers have more in common than you'd think, when it comes to relationships. *The Art of the Date* will show anyone how to make the most of their chemistry to enjoy lasting love and better sex at any income level.

Dating apps will not get you what you want. In fact, they're probably hurting your chances of finding true love. We wrote *The Art of the Date* to offer you a reliable, balanced approach to dating. No algorithms, no bullshit! We know our method works, and we have dozens of happy matches to prove it—including our own marriages.

We don't do rules, gimmicks, or weird pick-up lines. We just give it to you straight, from our experience. Love is life's biggest adventure—and best investment.

We wish you all the best in your search. We hope it will be the opportunity of a lifetime.

Sincerely,

Rori & Dr. Gluck

Chapter 1

Sexy Signals and the Zazazou

Any chemist will tell you that the reactions they create in the lab are anything but spontaneous. There's a method to it. The careful mixology that creates sparks, pizzazz, or even explosions depends on which chemicals are combined, and when, and how.

That's how people work, too. The right combination of two people can be magical. Effervescent. We call these power couples a *platinum pair*. They're strong, durable, and built on a connection that is truly priceless. The wrong combination of partners? We call that a nightmare! In making matches, we look carefully at the essential ingredients of each partner. We assess their desires, personality traits, and habits. Then, we can help people mingle and match more meaningfully. Think more sparkle, less sulphur. Those instantaneous connections can lead to more: love, meaningful bonds, commitment, and a future together. So what are the ingredients that make good dates happen?

In this chapter, we will help you assess what you bring to the table, what your personal chemistry is, and how to eliminate the behaviors that make you less appealing.

1

The Nose Knows

Dr. Gluck: The concept of "personal chemistry" is fascinating. Why are two people instantly drawn to one another? It's a phenomenon that is very much like perfume. It bewitches the senses, but eventually its scent fades away.

Rori: Are you saying there's more to love than a spritz of Hermès?

Dr. Gluck: Yes and no. Instant chemistry is that gut-level, instinctive attraction that two people have. It can't be bottled, or matching services and dating apps would be out of business! Chemistry is essential, but it's not a guarantee that the relationship will last or that you'll have it for more than a night.

Rori: For people looking for a meaningful match, it's OK to come across a little strong. Make your first impression a powerful one. That means finding a signature scent. Something that says *Hello, Mr. Big.*

If you smell like a cupcake, you're going to attract a baker, right? If you smell like a million bucks, you are going to send the signal that you're looking for a broker, a banker, or better yet, a millionaire. Many scents for women lean heavily on florals and vanilla scents. Those are good-girl smells. If that's who you are, then that's what you wear. If you're a bad girl, a heavier perfume will show your naughty streak.

Go to the perfume counter for guidance from an expert. Learn how muskier fragrances sit on your skin. For some people, especially those who want to be taken seriously, a heavy perfume is appropriate. Don't shy away from sandalwood, violet, or cashmere musks. Think of scent as a component of your outfit, too. If you're wearing a heavy-duty, super-feminine musk, that doesn't go with the yoga-pants-and-messy-bun look. You need to make sure you're picking a scent that promises something on which you can follow through. You're not fully dressed until you've applied your perfume with a dab or spritz in the places you want to be kissed: neck, cleavage, and the back of the knee. A little lipstick wouldn't kill you, either.

Perfume, like a good conversation, develops with your body heat. The scent can change, so be smart and pick something that will smell great after a two-hour dinner instead of leaving you smelling like yesterday's leftover salmon. A sure-fire, go-to perfume that is catnip for men is *Baiser Vole*, from Cartier. It's 100 percent lily. Versace *Crystal Noir* is a sexy, feminine evening scent. Another classic is Goutal, of course, which goes with everything.

What you want to do with perfume is invite someone to lean in a little closer—and not to take one sniff and say, *Wow, you smell like my grandma*. No, thanks! Work with a sales person to find something that's age appropriate and sends the right message.

For men, it's no different. A polished, herbal aftershave can fill in the gaps. Guys, it's better to go light on scents, since they can be overpowering and distracting. You don't want to be *That Guy* whose cologne is making the whole elevator stink like Pepe Le Pew! If I'm standing right next to a guy, that's the only time I should be able to smell him. Think clean and warm, like scents that contain bergamot or orange blossom. Dolce & Gabbana's *Pour Homme* is easy to wear and not too heavy. Keep away from unisex fragrances, or your date will think you're stepping out on another lady.

Dr. Gluck: Scents can trigger powerful memories. That's why perfume is key: your scent is linked to how your potential partner remembers you the day after your date. The sense of smell is part of our primal brain, so a person who is meeting you for the first time is going to pick up on the notes in your perfume. They may not realize it, but the subtle signals in your perfume are helping create this magical sense of chemistry between you.

Rori: You don't want to be linked in someone's mind to the smell of onion rings! Be intentional with your choices. It matters. Those initial chemistry signals tell both partners that something special is happening. My sense of chemistry with other people is all about romance: that instant click that makes me feel so good when I'm with them. I believe there is such a thing as a soulmate.

I feel everyone is meant to be with a certain kind of person, even if it's not forever—even if it's just for two weeks, or ten years. Chemistry can signal that you need that person during a particular time in your life. That's why we have all different kinds of people who come and go from our lives. They're with us for a reason, a season, or a lifetime. But the point is, it starts with the first date! And that first date had better be a good one.

Dr. Gluck: When you're with the right person, time flies! You don't get bored with the other person's company. You're fully enchanted. There is a feeling of sexual excitement coinciding with intellectual curiosity. You're on the same wavelength. When I met my first wife, it was in the middle of a college dance. I was out there being myself: sitting in the middle of the dance floor in my overalls with my legs folded. When my future wife spotted me, she leaned over to her best friend and said, "See that guy? I'm going to marry him."

And we *did* get married. We had a full life and raised two beautiful, intelligent daughters together. Our marriage ended when my wife passed away on January 5, 2001. She chose me based on her instantaneous attraction to me. We had chemistry, and it led to decades of love and mutual understanding. So, love at first sight does happen.

Rori: To me, chemistry is when a man touches me—on my arm, my face— and it just feels magical. The body, the smell, the touch, the brain, everything is working on overdrive. That's chemistry. It's definitely a strong starting point that suggests something deeper between people. Instantaneous lust can fold into love.

Body language can make or break a first impression. Guys have it a little easier, because they shake hands to say hello or goodbye. They're not expected to initiate physical contact like a hug. A guy, on a first date, needs to greet his partner with a friendly smile, a gentle touch on her shoulder or arm. His body language should be very respectful and convey that he is interested. A touch on the lower back, for example, as you're going to your table at the restaurant, is very sexy.

For women who are seriously looking for their perfect match, going over the top with touching isn't the way to go. I've heard of women flashing their new implants at a date, showing too much cleavage, or jumping straight into kissing when they've never even spent time with the guy! They definitely get the guy's attention, but the message they're sending is, *you can have all this and you don't have to earn it.* A woman who does that is a one-night stand waiting to

5

happen, and she will need to reel it in if she wants to find lasting love. A man who sees those signals and has easy access to your body is not going to respect you, and he's not going to perceive you as a serious match. He'll see a one-night stand, not the love of his life.

And that goes both ways, for men and women. If you want to get married, act like it. Dress like it. Put out those vibes that say *I'm marriage material*. Otherwise, you're better off playing the field and sparing yourself the effort and the heartbreak.

I say, keep it "classy sexy." A little skin, a little touch. You don't need to give the whole thing away to keep someone's attention. Part of chemistry is the mystery. It draws someone closer. You don't make that connection by stripping and jumping in the pool on the first date. Memorable? Sure. But I wouldn't want to take it to that level the first few months.

Chemistry isn't just a quality everyone has. It has to be cultivated. Think about it like this: if your soulmate comes up and taps you on the shoulder and he's wearing a hideous sweater and has the worst teeth you've ever seen and smells like capers, are you going to think, *yeah, that's the guy for me* or are you going to think twice? Everything about that moment is unappealing. The smell, the touch, the sweater. A man who is putting himself out there needs to consider how he's making the woman feel. He should be making her feel good, not making her hold her nose.

We are looking for love without compromise. Chemistry is that first positive reaction to someone. You shouldn't have to talk yourself off the ledge between the first and second dates or make up compromises in your head when you just met someone. You should feel butterflies! If you're thinking, *He's got a great smile, but oh my God, his whole wardrobe should go straight into the dumpster* then you're not in the moment. You're analyzing, not feeling. That's the opposite of romantic.

Dr. Gluck: Chemistry means you've found someone whose essence is complementary to yours, in some way. They've got the right stuff, and it grasps your attention.

To learn what makes up your personal chemistry, answer the questions below. In order to make the most of your personal attractiveness, you need to understand how you look on the outside, and what messages you're sending with your body language. Our beliefs are often mirrored in our gestures, clothing and grooming, and "unconscious" behaviors. Profile yourself by taking a look in the mirror— and at your partner, current or past. You can also work through these questions with a best friend, family member, or person you trust to be *completely honest* with you.

When you're answering these questions, keep in mind that you can assess your *current* relationship, any *past* relationship, or the relationship you'd like to have in the *future*.

> ➢ I believe my four best and four worst attributes are _____.
> ➢ My partner's four best and four worst attributes are _____.
> ➢ I can improve myself by _____.
> ➢ The chemistry in my relationship is _____.

➢ Right now, I most value
  _____.

➢ My favorite thing about myself is
  _____.

➢ People are attracted to me because
  _____.

Rori: Attraction must be more than skin deep. If
you don't have the physical, mental, and emotional
connections, then it's just infatuation, not love. The buck
stops with the initial attraction and that's it. The word *love* is
used all the time in our culture. But when we talk about
love, we have to define what it is—and isn't.

Chemistry is being drawn to the way the person
looks, sounds, and smells. All your senses are engaged. But
you don't yet know *who* he is. That's the mystery that
chemistry creates. It tempts you. You have to get to know
the person before you can love him. When you go through
a crisis with someone, you see how he or she reacts and it
provides insight into the person's character. When someone
is really down in the dumps and you're still there, that's
love.

Want to Socialize? Ditch Social Media!

Rori: Dating is a lost art. I hear so many people complain
that they're looking for a connection, but they can't seem to
find it. When someone says that, I ask them: where are you
looking? Every time, the story is the same. They are
desperately scrolling through dating apps, swiping, sending

messages. They think that's dating, but it's really shopping. Don't get me wrong, I love to shop too, but if I was spending top dollar on the biggest purchase of my life— bigger than a car, bigger than a home—you bet I wouldn't get it off Amazon. If you were buying a bespoke, designer handbag that you had to carry everywhere you went, every day, for the rest of your life, you would absolutely invest in it. And you wouldn't just buy it off the internet.

But that's what we do with relationships! We think we can pick some man or woman off the shelf and it'll all work out. A woman is not a *blender*. But I think it explains why relationships fail, that we look for love the same way we pick out a Vitamix. We actually work harder to learn about our gadgets and apparel than about the people who will become mainstays in our lives.

For some reason, people seem to think that love just comes along and falls into your lap. In reality, those matches and relationships are built from the bottom up. The scent, the touch. The way you look at someone. That's where love comes from.

I'm saying, chemistry and the magic of personal connections are being consumed by technology, social media, and dating apps. People genuinely desire connection, but often are so focused on phrasing the perfect text message that they forget to keep up their socializing abilities. They wear the bad sweater. They put on the unsexy shoes. Then, they meet someone face to face and flounder. Do the math: if you want to have chemistry, you've gotta get real!

Dr. Gluck: Modern people have misplaced the ability to read a person's expression or body language.

When it's time to go on a real, traditional date, they forget how to act. The art of conversation eludes them. They feel safer scrolling through their phones. Inductive reasoning goes out the window! Half the time, people don't even know how they feel because they're thrown into a new environment where they fail to observe anything. Dating is all about noticing what the other person is doing. In my study of profiling, I've noted that the initial chemistry, or the signs that cause someone to be attracted, are coded into their appearance and behavior. The same is true for the signs that communicate lack of attraction and will kill even the most intense chemistry. A person may look or smell appealing, but their actions say, "I'm not that into you." Some of the passive, unintentional behaviors that make chemistry evaporate are:

> Acting unfocused or distracted
> Wincing frequently, as though annoyed
> Leaning away from you
> Won't make eye contact
> Won't get physical in any way and refuses to hold hands, kiss, or touch
> Checking his or her phone to text, take calls, or answer emails

At the same time, a person can heighten their attractiveness and increase their chemistry by being aware of the positive messages they're sending. Looking someone in the eyes and smiling at them is a great way to show that you're interested in them—that you find them attractive. Yet, so many people miss out on those opportunities because they're looking at their phones.

As Rori said, touch is vital to building connections. If you're nervous around someone, it will show in your body language. If you are unsure of yourself and you put your hands in your pockets, that sends a message as well.

Rori: Let's face it: people are visual. Not just men! Most people are. We respond to so many factors that can't be communicated on a screen. Smells, touch, taste. There isn't a phone on the market that can give me the feeling I get when my husband hugs me. Technology can't replace that.

Say you receive a text message from someone you're seeing that says, *I love you.* Maybe there's even a red heart at the end of it. But are those three words what the other person really feels? You don't have a clue. They're just words. And they leave *you* reading between the lines, looking for information that will help you make a decision to move forward or not.

The problem with social media and technology is that they create the illusion of chemistry. It's just part of the whole picture, though. You might think there's a connection that seems powerful and right, only to be confronted with reality when you meet in person. Their picture looked great, or their message was perfectly crafted, but there's no chemistry at all.

Dr. Gluck: When it comes to dating, technology has made us myopic.

Rori: Yes, and that's why dating apps are only partially successful. These days, 30 percent of marriages begin online. That sounds like a lot, but when you consider that Platinum Poire has an extremely high success rate for happy, long term relationships, it's clear that our method works better. Simply matching online via an algorithm isn't working for 70 percent of the people who are looking for love.

People try to play matchmaker for themselves and it doesn't work because they're too shy, don't know how they come across to others, or have unrealistic expectations. The good news is, we can fix those issues. The bad news is, you have to be willing to change your ways.

The Platinum Poire agency method requires a totally honest assessment of your body, your personal habits, and your body language. We can look at a person and see exactly what's holding them back from having the relationship of their dreams. If you are looking in the mirror and saying, *But I have a beautiful personality*, then you are missing the point. Your exterior should represent your interior self. We have a culture now that seems to think that the average person should have to dig deep to discover your special qualities, but I'm saying, if you expect people to overlook your crooked teeth or the extra weight you're hauling around, you are living in a dream world. Most people, open-minded or not, make snap decisions based on what they see.

They see the teeth, or the unbalanced figure, and they aren't attracted. The good news is, those are things that can be corrected. You can go to the orthodontist and get your smile straightened. You can commit to the gym and put some tone on your body. You can spend a little money on a nutritionist, who can give you a meal plan and a weekly shopping list, so you aren't living on frozen dinners or fast food. This stuff isn't rocket science, but people who are hoping for a match can't treat self-care like it's optional. You know how to lose that twenty pounds, so go do it.

Ideally, you will look and feel like your best self. That will shine out and attract someone who's proud to be seen with you: not someone who's settling, or who won't take the relationship seriously. Show your worth, and you will be valued.

> What is your best physical feature?

> What is your least attractive physical feature?

> Do you ever think, "If it wasn't for _____, I would go on more dates"? What's preventing you from changing?

> What makes you feel sexy and attractive?

Fashion Is Foreplay

Rori: If you're not camera-ready, you're not ready! Women definitely have the upper hand in the art of looking glam. We have a history of knowing how to wax, laser, curl, cream, primp, and present ourselves in a particular way from a very early age. We check each other out and give each other constant feedback about what looks good and what doesn't. A friend who won't tell you what she honestly thinks of your outfit is *not* your friend.

Fashion is like pro football for women. We compete at it, watch designers and trends, and we *absolutely* assess every little detail. But that doesn't mean we're going to let guys off the hook!

One thing women know that men are *finally* figuring out is that fashion is foreplay. The way you dress, smell, style yourself, whatever. This is the visual first move you make on a person. Before you even open your mouth, your clothes are doing the talking. The way your ass looks in those jeans, or the perfect fit of his shirt, is immediately sexy. Just the right amount of cleavage; the bare shoulder; fabrics that hug the body or add softness—every detail matters. So guys, you are *not* allowed to wear sweatpants if you're on your way to meet your soulmate. Unless you're Alex Rodriguez, straight out of practice, with a black card in your pocket for me to take you shopping, I forbid it!

A woman looks at three things when she meets a man for the first time: his shoes, his package, and his watch. In that order! Don't think we are keeping our eyes to ourselves, guys. That means that, if you're a man, you need to make sure you're wearing nice, clean shoes when you leave the house. You talk to your tailor and make sure your pants fit in the front. No pleats, please. And wear a watch that says you're an adult man with a big-boy job and a real paycheck—no calculator watches, no pocket watches, and no Fitbits. Your accessories should show that you can and do take care of yourself. If you wore it in college, it's probably time to retire it. You need to send the message that you're successful—not living in the dorms with your buddies or crashing in your parents' spare bedroom.

The clothes really do make the man! Many men who are smart, successful, and even confident simply do not know how to convey that message in their appearance. It undermines their desire to be coupled with beautiful, stylish women. What glamorous woman would want to go out

14

with a guy who looks like he shops for all his clothes at once, once a year, at Costco? Hell no!

You don't have to be a clotheshorse or a male model but making a line item in your personal budget for clothing and a tailor is key. Most department stores, and even the online clothing subscription services, have personal stylists who can work with your budget to give you a great look.

Guys have it easy in some ways. *Any* effort is a good thing. A little extra time, money, and research, especially with a personal shopper or a *GQ* style guide, will go a long way with women.

Dr. Gluck: It's very common to see a man who lacks any sense of style struggling to find a date. This is often the case with very smart men. But Rori has a great sense of style, so she gives the man advice from head to toe, literally. She fixes the external stuff, and I fix the internal problems.

Rori: The inside and outside definitely work together to create a whole picture of the person. Let's say a woman comes to us who doesn't take great care of herself, but she's interested in meeting some Adonis who is perfectly toned, taut, and doesn't have a spare ounce of fat on his body. She wants a man who takes good care of himself, even though she does not: she needs to drop twenty pounds. This reason this woman will have more difficulty being matched is because her expectations are unrealistic. She expects Mister Olympia to just fall head over heels for her, when clearly, their values are very different. A man like that is going to be deeply invested in physical culture, very aware of looks and diet. It's written all over his perfect body. And he's probably not going to be excited to date someone or commit to someone whose values are not aligned with his. Also, how happy would she be, eating celery and protein shakes every night instead of snuggling up with some takeout and a good movie? It's just not a fit.

It's one thing to fantasize—we all do it, and it's healthy!—but if you want to be happy, you need to be honest about what *you* bring to the table. This is where you need an honest outside perspective. If you have things you need to fix, fix them. Don't make excuses and expect other people to give you a pass. Be your best self, at all times.

Dr. Gluck: If you lack something, you have to have enough humility to get support. Most problems or shortcomings are solvable. Genuine self-confidence is immensely attractive. When you're confident, nothing bothers you. But if your ego has been continually bruised, you're probably not ready to follow through on an attraction to another person. Being in a relationship is like running a marathon. If you can't even walk a block without tripping over your feet, don't try to run a marathon. Get some help.

Rori: It is important for you to be honest with yourself regarding what you can and can't fix. At Platinum Poire, what we do is help people see themselves. Get a clear picture of who you are, what you care about, and what you're working with. I'll give you a tip: there is usually more good stuff than you think. Realistic expectations are not your enemy. They're the key to success, to sustaining attraction, and turning it into something meaningful.

My focus is on how people portray themselves on the outside. If you're tired of your style and need to change it a little bit, I can refine you from head to toe. When

16

you're looking for love, you are your own walking business card. Just like in business, you have to bring your A-game in order to seal the deal. Some people just need to bring out their inner goddess and help get their groove back! Frequently, prospective Platinum Poire members have been in a long-term relationship rut: they got comfortable, fat, and emotionally lazy. It's easy to fall in love. The hardest part is staying in love. New relationship, new and better version of you!

When it comes to enhancing your appearance, we connect our clients with some of the top skincare professionals, doctors, or dentists in New York that cater to the power players. Enhancements can be as minimal as recommending a great hair stylist to recommending veneers or plastic surgery. Love is not for the faint of heart and you have to work for it.

Our desire at Platinum Poire is for you to be healthy inside and out to get ready for that special relationship. Once you are, you can attract what you want.

We're fortunate in that Platinum Poire has a choice of who becomes our clientele. We have to believe in them, assess their personal chemistry, and feel we can make a positive difference in their lives. Expectations are key, as well as understanding what the client brings to the table.

Our goals don't always match, of course. A potential client called me recently. She was a successful and beautiful woman in her mid-forties. However, she was *very* adamant about the "physical type" of man she was looking to date. She described her ideal partner as "very tall, younger than her, and Italian stallions only."

17

I said, "Honey, I'm not taking him for a test drive—neither is my assistant, and certainly not my male partner, Dr. Gluck. Listen, this is not Tinder."

We were not a match professionally. Platinum Poire strives to make matches that last a lifetime. And those all start with chemistry—not hard and fast rules. That's why we do create a checklist and work with the clients to establish a set of do's and don'ts. Relationships need to be nurtured from that initial spark, and they all play by their own rules. Who wants to tame love or put love in a cage? Not me.

Dr. Gluck: Neuroplasticity, which is a major aspect of my practice, is a great tool to create and maintain chemistry. It is a means to greater freedom of choice. A patient's mind may be blocked because they hold different beliefs or fears about themselves. For example, you may have been deeply invested in a relationship that recently fell apart. You think about the person you lost constantly. You worry that you'll never find someone like that again, and you compare every new potential date with the person you're obsessing over. Yet, even when this non-stop thinking becomes harmful to you—to your self-esteem, your future with another person, and your happiness—you can't stop. You can't turn off those thoughts. Hypnosis can enable you to change your thought process, so this person is on your mind for just a few seconds every six months instead of taking up every channel, twenty-four/seven.

Hypnosis is not manipulation. It's about rewiring the thought process and changing it from emotional and destructive, to rational and productive; getting past intellectual and emotional blockages that are a part of who you are. Your brain actually reinterprets your experience. That includes recovering from a broken heart. So many people crave connection and will come to Platinum Poire saying that they are ready to find Mister or Miss Right. In reality, they're on guard. They're not really open. They're terrified of rejection.

But all rejection is actually self-rejection. Look at it like this: would your keys start my car or open the door to my house? Nope. They don't fit the lock. They weren't made to open any door except the one that was designed for *you*. If you can't get into *my* house with *your* keys, it isn't a rejection of you. It's just not a fit, and you can't take it personally.

From there, it's a process of understanding ourselves with new acceptance and better expectations. Nothing is personal. Rejection isn't about us. It just indicates it wasn't meant to be.

> ➤ What am I really looking for in a relationship?
> ➤ What type of person is the best fit for my personality?
> ➤ What are my deal-breakers, and can I stick to them?

Rori: The majority of the divorced women I interview tell me that what they want a bad boy. The power broker in the bespoke suit, big Rolex, private plane. They want a real estate tycoon who is rich, romantic, and just happens to be a non-committal player. But these ladies

19

are forty-five, divorced, and ultra-successful with children to support. Many of them are craving the feeling of being a wild child. They want to hop on a private jet with that bad boy and fly off into the sunset.

If they do find this kind of guy, he'll know how to wine them and dine them. He might even fly them to Paris for the weekend at a moment's notice. But then, you never know when you'll hear from him again. He's actually a mysterious commitment-phobe who may or may not have a different girl in his bed every night. This package is crazy-spontaneous, comes with gifts and zero commitment, and is guaranteed to make you nuts. We do not offer this at Platinum Poire.

The women who go after this kind of guy are hoping to get the leopard to change his spots. *Come on.* It's a recipe for disaster. The bad boy was cute when you were twenty-five, but two decades later? It's an expiration date waiting to happen.

We all know women who haven't grown up inside, and they crave that wild action. Maybe their marriage was really conservative, or they want to cut loose after their divorce. Maybe their husband left them for a younger woman and they're looking for a revenge fuck. They associate bad boys with the fun of being irresponsible. I say, *OK, you can get that in a weekend in Ibiza.*

Let's say that she *does* find the bad boy of her dreams. Let's say it lasts more than a weekend! Let's say that he doesn't cheat on her (which would be a miracle). If they stay together for a decade and then split, she's now fifty-five. It is much more difficult to pick up the pieces at that age and start over without compromise. Your relationship expectations can, and should, be very different from the sexy, animal chemistry that rubs you the right way in the moment.

Relationships are long term, lifetime investments. It might sound counterintuitive, but when you get into a relationship, you should be thinking about the relationships that comes *after* the one you're currently in. How will this set you up for the next partner?
If you don't plan to stay together with someone for life—or even if you do—it's very important to consider what kind of condition you'll be in if your current relationship ends.

Some of the questions you could ask yourself are:

> How long do I usually stay in serious relationships?
> How old will I be when this relationship expires?
> What will I need in terms of love, connection, and support in five years? Does my current partner provide that?
> If my type doesn't change, can I adapt to keep attracting that kind of person?

Again, realistic goals and a solid understanding of who you are, inside and out, will help you feel fulfilled in a partnership with someone who can give you what you need.

Dr. Gluck: It speaks to the power of chemistry that people are willing to trade safety for the adventure of love. They jump in head first, and never stop to consider that things might end badly. People are driven to create connections with one another, no matter what the outcome may be. But it doesn't have to end in tears if you do a little planning and some preparation before you make that phone call or give that person your card.

Love can happen any time. Sustaining the initial attraction happens when you put in the work to continually reinvent yourself. If you can come to the relationship with a strong sense of self, and with the ability to show tremendous support and patience toward your partner, then you're on the way to a successful, life long partnership. Taking the time to analyze your strengths and weaknesses is the beginning of a vested interest in your growth and your future.

Love finds a way, but you do need to participate and encourage it to develop. When you're ready to move beyond the magic of chemistry, and you've got the tools you need to grow, your chances of beating the statistics are substantial. You can be in the percentage of people who link up for life and find marriages and partnerships worth keeping.

Chapter 2

Sexual Attraction Is More Than Skin Deep

Sex is power. And power is sexy! Sex is the seductive suggestion underneath all that personal chemistry. Even people, like Barry Diller and Diane von Furstenberg, who don't look like models or movie stars can have powerful sexual charisma that draws others to them. Many platinum pairs—from George and Amal Clooney to Tom Brady and Gisele Bündchen—are undeniably attractive. *He's got it. She's so sexy. They're so hot together.*

Sex puts the "power" in "power couple." It can draw people together or push them apart. Just like chemistry, sexiness is magnetic. In platinum pairs, there's no denying that sex is vital. Testing your sexual compatibility is imperative. A partner who checks all the boxes *except* your sexual needs is going to be a dud, long-term. To find love without compromise, you need and deserve a partner who satisfies you, in and out of the bedroom. There are some areas you don't concede—this is one of them.

Sex is not always a subject we bring up on a first date. Or the fifth, or sixth date! We may be intensely sexually attracted to someone, but not know if we're really compatible with them. Our sexual appetites may not match our relationship expectations. In a relationship, we don't

23

compromise, we synchronize. It is possible to have both, in one package.

In this chapter, Dr. Gluck and Rori will help you assess your personal sexual preferences, your sex drive, and your needs. It's been said that "if things aren't working in the bedroom, they won't work anywhere else." You deserve to be satisfied with your partner, and the way to get there is by making sure you pick a partner who really knows how to make you melt beneath the sheets.

Raise Your Sexpectations

Rori: Chemistry and sex are intimately connected. Sex comes up at every stage of dating, but we may handle it a little differently as we grow in our relationships. The crazy, passionate one-night stand energy may not last for more than a night. However, I know couples that have kept that flame burning over months, years, and even decades. They make it work because they know that sex is essential. Sexpectations are good for relationships!

Sexuality, emotions, and our psychological makeup can either work to help you find a match or prevent you from achieving what you desire. They're deeply intertwined. Remember that a marriage is cemented in bed—so get down to business!

Dr. Gluck: Throughout our lives, we'll all have various types of relationships that can add—or detract—from our experience. A good relationship can provide a more fulfilling and prosperous, healthier, and happy life. In my practice, I've worked with clients who have been sexually abused or assaulted. It's natural that they'd have problems with intimacy.

24

Many people struggle to understand their sexuality. They may have been sexually hurt in the past. A previous relationship may have left them feeling inadequate or unfulfilled. Those sexual wounds can stay with us for years, or even decades. Yet, many people are slow to address sex because it's so closely tied to their identities. Intimacy, which is the exploration of the chemistry between two people, can help you open up about sex.

Remember, even people who have significant trauma around sex can walk through those issues and overcome them. And those people who have never experienced trauma have a much easier time moving through their fears and coping with sexual inadequacy. We all have some insecurities. Regardless of what you may have been through, you can have relationships that are whole and nurturing, too.

Rori: If you have had serious sex issues or trauma, seek the help of a therapist. Just like you'd go to a professional for skincare or toothache. You need to fix your inner self, too. There's no point in spending hundreds, or thousands, on making your outside look great if you aren't actually in a place to date mentally. It's a waste of your effort, and it will let down anyone who's a potential match. It's false advertising.

If you know that you are commitment-phobic, or you're still healing from a bad situation in your past, there are wonderful therapists who can help you work through it. You'll be doing yourself and everyone else a favor. Don't set yourself up for disappointment because you're unwilling or fearful to deal with any issues that may be inhibiting you.

What's between your ears affects what happens between your legs!

Dr. Gluck: Sex can hurt, and it can heal too. It's satisfying to have sex with someone you love. It provides a sense of completeness. But some individuals can simply have sex for the sake of pleasure, no strings attached. Sex is a physical feeling that creates powerful emotions. It does not necessarily lead to a meaningful bond. There's a common saying that men think with their small head, not their big head. Women do this too! They don't think, they act.

Rori: Like I said before, if you want to get married, act like it. Do you envision your future wife as someone who gets naked on the first date? Or ladies, do you want to marry a guy who expects sex after one candlelit dinner? *Nope.* Lasting partnerships happen between people who respect each other and respect the power of sex. It's not something you do lightly, when you're looking for love that lasts.

Think before you jump into bed, especially in the beginning. It's better to hold back and see someone's true colors, rather than act and regret. It takes time to build something meaningful. That's why dating is so important. It gives you the chance to explore your initial attraction to one another and see whether the chemistry is the real deal.

Keep your sexpectations high by noticing how the other person acts, what they say, and how they share their values. You do not need to compromise, but you do need to give someone a chance to show you with what they are working. Feel it out. See if you are attracted, beyond your

26

mutual chemistry. If it's not a fit after three dates, move on to the next.

Trust me, you won't cry yourself to sleep at night over *not* sleeping with someone but falling into bed too soon is a recipe for regret. You will never, ever feel sorry for respecting yourself. In the end, that's what really matters.

Kiss Me, or Miss Me?

Dr. Gluck: Nothing is worse than good chemistry that falls flat in the bedroom. So, how do we predict sexual compatibility? We use the oldies but goodies: how someone smells, and how it feels to kiss them.

The magic of kisses and a person's scent come from pheromones. Those are the natural chemicals that your body gives off, which can change the way other people perceive you. Pheromones send signals about your hormones, such as whether you're sexually aroused, about to menstruate, or feeling stressed or territorial. In humans, there is some evidence that hormones influence attraction. This is beyond a good cologne or visual signals, like a nice suit. It's deeper, affecting the part of the brain that doesn't recognize an Hermès tie but *definitely* knows a powerful, sexy man.

We sense others' pheromones through our olfactory glands, by smelling. They're powerful, but subtle. You don't sniff someone and immediately jump on their lap. But someone's individual pheromones have an undeniable influence on your attraction to them. Humans' pheromone-influenced behavior pattern may not be as cut and dried as in other species, but it's present, even in sophisticated people with a highly developed social awareness.

That's why there's no denying that rubbing noses is a surefire way to test compatibility.

Rori: You can't be 100 percent sure until you do the deed. Sex isn't the first test that someone needs to pass, though. Remember that the first date is the *audition*. The second date tends to be a bit more relaxed. By the third date, both people should be comfortable enough to expose themselves—in more ways than one!

With sex, especially if you're getting back into dating after a divorce or a long time on your own, it's normal to need a little time to be by yourself. That wall may not come down right away. The other person might be moving at the same pace, so be patient. As you relax, you'll also be able to see whether the other person is actually someone you would like to get to know in a relationship.

Of course, the kiss will tell it *all*. Bad kiss, bad chemistry.

What makes a good kiss? Romance, of course. The kiss should not begin on the lips, just as attraction begins with a look or a feeling. Every kiss is an exploration, especially that first time. In a good kiss, the lips are the destination, not the starting point. The hand is a safe spot to begin. You might also kiss someone on the neck, depending on your chemistry with them.

Dr. Gluck: There are naturals in every facet of life, even kissing. There are also people a little disconnected from their body. Can they be taught to use their mouth, tongue and hands, and body? Yes. An awkward kiss is not the same thing as a bad kiss. If your connection is good, you can build on that to have better sex together.

Before You Unzip, Are You Ready to Bare It All?

Rori: An emotional bond is a bare-minimum requirement for sex. It's the initial investment of a relationship. Bonding should be a no-brainer, but for some reason people think they can skip that step and still end up with a fairy-tale ending. Reality check, please!

Most of the women I interview say they need an emotional connection with their date. Something, anything! This isn't reality TV, where people couple up within hours of meeting. It's your life.

No matter what you see on TV and on dating shows, most people prioritize emotions over time between the sheets. Women generally aren't interested in sex just for sex—and plenty of men aren't, either. Again, if you're searching for your soulmate, you're going to be looking beyond the superficial stuff. You want someone who makes you feel good: that person you want to see at the end of a long, difficult day, with whom you feel comfortable being yourself. Sexual passion may keep you warm for a night, but it doesn't provide the fuel for a lasting relationship.

Now, that was certainly true for me. The man that I am happily married to today is not my first husband. Like many people, I had a "starter marriage" when I was very young. I want to be clear that I have the utmost respect for my first husband and for the years we spent together. I don't regret the marriage, because it gave me my first son, whom I adore and is the light of my life. However, that partnership was very much built on sexual attraction. We were both so young, and we didn't know what we were doing. We confused sex with love and ended up having to

29

separate because the foundation of a mature, lasting relationship just wasn't there.

In my second marriage, I'm experiencing what it means to really be loved—as a woman, a mother, a partner, an equal. My husband complements me. He's the kind of guy who can go the distance with me. We're very attracted to each other, and that attraction is supported by the fact that we have so much mutual respect. It's healthy. Sex isn't our primary way of bonding, making up after fights, or communicating how we feel about each other. We do that in other ways. He's the perfect match for me, and while sex is a priority for us, it's not the only thing holding us together.

Got the message? Bottom line, sex is not a shortcut. You can't fuck your way to true love. An emotional bond means that you and your partner have spent time together. You've gotten intimate and put some of your cards on the table. You've taken the time to understand one another. You're genuinely ready to take the next step.

Dr. Gluck: Just as we can't create a connection from chemistry that isn't there, we can't put a couple of strangers together and expect them to have great sex. People are not pandas. Creating a match based only on superficial factors would be unrealistic and irresponsible. Yet people do that to themselves all the time when they're trying to find a partner. They hook up, have casual sex, and then wonder why the one-night stand didn't turn into something more. *How* you have sex, and with whom, is a great predictor of whether you'll end up partnered or perpetually searching for someone to love.

My personal belief is that emotional intimacy is necessary before sexual intimacy can have any meaning. Sex for its own sake connects to the animalistic part of the brain. In many cases, sex can be destructive. On the other hand, sex can be healthy and affirming. Sex can release tension within the body and can also improve your mood. It's a muscular release and a validation of desirability, as long as it isn't in conflict with your personal or spiritual values.

Listening and communication skills are the bare minimum for good sexual connection. If you're simply submitting to the other person out of fear of losing them, then you're compromising your values. Know yourself and know your partner. Each partner's desires, needs, and boundaries must be learned, respected, and fulfilled in order to have a successful relationship.

Put Your Sex Drive in Gear

Rori: You probably have a good idea about your own sexuality. If you've been around the block, you should know whether your sex drive is low or high or somewhere in between. You're not new to sex, so even if you're open to new things, you have probably figured out what you like, what you can't stand, and what makes you want to kick someone straight out of bed.

Especially if you're dating after divorce, you might have gotten sexually complacent. You might have felt ignored or neglected. You might have cheated, or been cheated on, because the relationship didn't provide sexual satisfaction. Often, marriages fail because someone's needs aren't being met. The same three positions, sex at the same

31

time of day, or mismatched sexual appetites can really wear a relationship down. Who wants that?

The good news is, when you're dating new people, you can experience the kind of sex you want to have. Never settle when you're selecting a new partner. Want to know if you'll be a match in the bedroom? Notice what kind of chemistry your date is putting out there. Do his signals say "50 Shades of Player" or "Mister Vanilla"? And, on the flip side, do *your* signals match your desires, too?

Dr. Gluck: Many dating apps don't even bring sex into the picture, which is another reason that they don't work. Your personal approach to sex is very important. A relationship that doesn't consider your preferences, values, and desires is not one you'll want to keep. You can explore your sexual identity by answering these questions. They are based on the profile process we use at Platinum Poire.

➢ For me, sex is _____.

➢ I like having sex _____ times a week/month/year.

➢ For sex to be enjoyable, I must have _____.

➢ Am I comfortable with nudity? Lights on or lights off?

➢ Do I like my body?

➢ What are my expectations about sex?

➢ Am I comfortable with non-sexual touch? Do I enjoy hugging and kissing? Do I like to cuddle?

➢ For me, fidelity is _____.

➤ Is infidelity a deal breaker?

➤ How do I express affection? What forms of affection are my favorites?

➤ Am I kinky? How do I feel about threesomes, fetishes, same-sex experiences, or trying new things? Am I open to one-night stands?

➤ Do I climax easily?

➤ What was my best sexual experience and why?

➤ What is the most important aspect of sex for me?

➤ Is sex a form of communication for me or a physical activity?

➤ Do I need an emotional connection in order to have sex? How much intimacy do I need before I have sex with someone new?

Rori: Be honest with yourself about what works for you and what turns you off. Don't sell yourself short. This is the *one* area of your life where you should not settle! Remember that you're looking for a relationship that will last, with a partner you are excited to come home to every night.

When Your Maybe-Mate is Not a Match

Dr. Gluck: Platinum Poire's high success rate comes from our honest assessment of each person, their needs, and their ideal relationship outcome. Our matches thrive because we are realistic about love. The fact is, there's more to marriage than fantasy. Being realistic about with whom you really belong, and who's good for you, is hard for some people.

Rori: The age-old question: *Do opposites attract?*

Dr. Gluck: We hear that question all the time.

Rori: And as Dr. Gluck and I both say, *Yes, they attract, but they'll eventually rip each other apart.* Opposites can be exciting in the short term, but they spell disaster in a romantic relationship. It'll never last. Of course, try telling that to someone who deeply believes that they belong with somebody who is nothing like them.

Dr. Gluck: Opposites attract, and then they kill each other. You need enough of an opposite to create what I call *creative tension.* Creative tension is sustained chemistry. It's when you sense a connection with someone and put in the work to keep that feeling going. You play with that chemistry. It's sexy and exciting, even in long term relationships. It gives the feeling that your partner is always new, even if you've known them for years. Creative tension maintains sexual excitement, curiosity, and interest in a relationship. If chemistry is the spark in the relationship, creative tension is its daily fuel.

From a practical standpoint, that means that opposites may work in the bedroom—but not for long. As a man, you may think it's exciting to be with a very young, innocent girl. Her lack of experience contrasts with your own. But is that what you ultimately really want? The way that dynamic affects the rest of your relationship will make you both very unhappy. Being someone's "first" everything creates so much pressure. It places a heavy responsibility on you. Also, there's more to a partnership than just sex. There are financial decisions, family, raising children together, and going through all of life's changes. Sustaining a real, meaningful, mature relationship with someone who has no life experience is draining. All the fun you were having disappears! For a man who was very attached to his fantasy, we might encourage him to find a partner who's physically attractive to him and enjoys role-play.

Rori: If someone's not a fit, don't keep trying to fit a square peg in a round hole. The first three dates should tell you all you need to know, in order to decide whether you want to move forward or not. There's a time when very different personality types are ideal together, but it's usually in platonic relationships. You know, coworkers, friends, collaborators, and business partners. Sex is counterproductive in those relationships because they are not about, well, sex!

Maybe you meet someone with whom you really love spending time or talking, but they don't have that special something. They don't give you butterflies. The romantic aspect of the date falls flat. That's fine: you've met a friend, not your future husband. It's not a reflection on either of you. It's just not a fit. Put him in the friend zone and find a new date.

Dr. Gluck: The age-old question is, can men and women be friends? It's possible that you'll meet many wonderful people while you're dating. You may even sleep with someone and realize later that you're better off as friends. Be honest, be kind, and have a conversation with them that enables you both to move on.

Rori: To some degree, dating is a numbers game. Think about it: if you're looking for "The One," you don't stop looking until you've found that person is who right for you. Simple. Now, let's assume that your soulmate is your hundredth date. That means you go on ninety-nine dates before you find "The One." From a numbers perspective, you have a 1 percent success rate, because one out of the one hundred people was your perfect match. From a Platinum Poire perspective, you have a 100 percent success rate, because you did two things right. First, you found a relationship in which you can believe and to which you choose commit, with someone that makes you happy. Second, you didn't settle for Mister Number Ninety-eight. You kept going until you matched with someone you could love without compromise. You were patient and didn't compromise.

Those ninety-nine dates are worth your time to find your soulmate. Most people don't need to look for that long to find their special match. Just keep in mind that you can't find "the One" if you're holding onto something that is not totally working for you. Why sell yourself short? You deserve real love.

Bonding Outside the Bedroom

Dr. Gluck: Building trust and working through sexual issues creates better relationships, which leads to better sex. It's not complicated! Most people simply don't know how to be patient or ask the right questions.

Rori: Okay, I'll say this again: if you want to be more than a one-night stand, or even a one-month stand, act like it. Who is this person you're dating? What are they like? How do they really fit into your life? The emotional roots of a relationship must be established before you even *think* about getting serious in bed. Sex is a powerful force and throwing it into the mix too early can turn a promising beginning into a total train wreck.

Dr. Gluck: Sexual imbalance and sexual incompatibility are red flags. Your life should be balanced in ways that make you feel healthy. Internal and external, body and mind. Committing to your own happiness is a big step for people who are looking for love. Good sex is the natural outcome of a healthy, sustained connection between two people who are drawn to one another. It happens at the right time for *both* people. Your ideal match isn't your opposite: it's someone who makes you really feel like yourself.

Rori: It's smart to wait to have sex. Once you cross that bridge, you can't go back. Drawing out the first part of your relationship, getting to know someone, is always worth your time. Kissing on dates is fine. It's a way of getting to know each other. It opens the door for more intimacy.

Once sex is on the table, things do start to change. Even if it's good sex! Even great sex can destroy a developing relationship. Sex can end up being so addictive that you begin thinking like a teenager. You lose your perspective, and you might end up with someone who is really only good in that one area of the relationship. If you are a highly sexual person, you may end up chasing that feeling forever, that results in wasting years of your life. You may run through dozens of "opposites" before you're able to find the person who has the right combination of sexiness and substance for you.

This is a hard limit for me: I say, no sex on the first date. *No way.* You and your date don't know each other. It's a recipe for disaster. A relationship must be built on a foundation of friendship. No matter how tempting it is, don't do it. It's too risky, and it sets you up for heartbreak. Look, I'm the kind of person where I know myself: I'm a person who really believes in respect. Not only do I give it to myself, I also demand it from a significant other. I don't want to worry about sleeping with a guy and then he doesn't call me the next day. I wouldn't expect some stranger to know that about me, but after three dates or more? He would definitely know what my priorities are and how to make me feel special.

Dr. Gluck: Taking time also ensures that the sex you have with a new partner is better for both of you. If you've experienced unfulfilling sex in the past, ask yourself *why* it was unfulfilling. Did it feel good to you, but your partner wasn't impressed? Is it a performance issue, or just a lack of practice?

The worst sex is when you are trying to perform. This is why many men suffer from erectile dysfunction, and why both men and women feel pressure to fake their orgasms. They think it is a performance. They lack trust in their partners, and that absence of emotional support and mutual reliance undermines their sexual experience.

Rori: When your mouth is screaming *yes, yes!* but your brain is screaming *no, no!* it usually means you skipped a step. You put sex before intimacy, or you decided to compromise your ideals in order to have a quickie on the beach. That's fine, but don't have great expectations for the relationship to pan out. There are no shortcuts to finding your soulmate.

Dr. Gluck: If you feel stuck or overwhelmed, look at the list of questions we provided earlier in the chapter. Take the time to work out your responses. If you're excited to share your answers with the person you're dating and hear what they have to say, that's a good sign that you're emotionally ready to get into bed.

The best time to share your answers with the person you're dating is right after the best experience you have together: when you are laughing, loving, and playing. Don't be a college professor or therapist. You don't need to give a lecture, draw a diagram, or unpack all your baggage. Show your fun-loving, enthusiastic side to the person sitting across (or on top) of you.

Mommies, Daddies, and Babies

Rori: Like you need another reason to use your head, remember that everyone has *issues*. I'm a big believer that most men have mommy issues. They need validation from a woman. Most women have daddy issues. It's just the way it is. When you jump into bed with someone, you're going to be encountering their expectations about the opposite sex. Are they looking for a mommy? A daddy? Find out *before* you do the deed.

For me, I've always loved older men and I have a good relationship with my father. I've never been attracted to younger guys. After my divorce, younger guys came out of nowhere, and I was like, *get out of here. You're a child! Go away.* They were like babies to me, and I wanted a husband who could make me feel loved, protected, and provided for. I craved that safety I feel with a mature male presence. Younger men couldn't give me that, so I didn't date them.

39

That's why, elsewhere in my life, I have a male trainer, doctor, hair stylist—I feel good in the care of men. Dr. Gluck and I, for example, complement one another in a supportive, productive way. He started out as my mentor, and then supported me as I evolved into his business partner and the face of Platinum Poire. He's older than I— I won't tell you by how much! The point is, we balance one another. We work well together. We are also both happily married to other people!

Dr. Gluck: The younger woman/older man dynamic is fairly common. This is one of the issues on which I work with clients. Why do younger women like older men? Why do older men like younger women? We try to match people who will grow together, not just put up with each other. That means acknowledging the individual's needs. We aren't trying to change anyone. We do examine the motive of someone who's seeking a particular type of relationship. For example, if our client is an older man who's looking for a significantly younger partner, he may be driven by a desire for her youth or naiveté. A younger woman who is only considering wealthy, much older men, might be motivated by money. Platinum Poire creates successful pairs because we know that the relationship needs to be built on more than these superficial desires.

Rori: Any time there's a "trade" in the relationship's dynamic, I don't see it working out long term. There has to be more substance for a lasting relationship. There's a difference between being drawn to older men and roping in yourself a sugar daddy. Or, from the other side, does the guy want a sugar baby because it strokes his ego? Does he get off on having the youngest wife at the party?

You can have a very happy marriage between people of vastly different ages. It's a personal decision, and it's all about the dynamic. For example, what about a divorced, financially successful father. He's got a couple of grown children in college. He's a CEO who travels and goes to important functions. Who's a good match for him? Probably not a very young woman, without an education, who hasn't traveled or experienced life. That man is going to need a partner who's smart, a dynamo. He's not shopping for arm candy.

If one person or both are being materialistic, the relationship will run its course really fast. Maybe a couple of years, at best. Mutual respect has to be built. We love that instant gratification but searching for the person who's going to essentially provide a service or a quick fix is actually working *against* your bigger goal of finding a life partner.

Two is Company, Three's a Crowd

Dr. Gluck: In the questions shared earlier in the chapter, we included a very important question—about infidelity. Now, infidelity and cheating are not the same as non-monogamy. When you answered this question, you should have defined what infidelity means to you. Believe it or not, not everyone has the same concept of faithfulness. When you are dealing with an infidelity issue, your initial reaction will be pain or anger. Look beyond your own emotions for a moment and determine what you can live with and what you can tolerate. If you've been cheated on in the past, consider that situation as well, since it will inform your boundaries for your future relationship. Ask yourself several questions:

> How will you feel about your partner's infidelity if you continue in the relationship?

> Does the infidelity impact the trust you have in that person?

> Is the infidelity something you might throw in the other person's face the next time you disagree or argue?

> Are your feelings something that will fester inside you?

> Are you the type of person who obsesses about incidents from the past? In other words, are you likely to lie awake at night and imagine your partner's sexual encounter in excruciating detail? Or could you let it go?

If your definition of infidelity isn't flexible, or if you wouldn't be able to forgive someone for cheating, stay away from partners whose idea of faithfulness includes sex with other people. Again, their choices are never a reflection on you. Nor should you pretend to have the kind of personality that is totally open and doesn't put limits on sex. Healthy boundaries mean better decisions, which leads to healthier relationships.

The most vital component in mastering any facet of the art of dating is honesty about yourself, what you're looking for, your boundaries, needs, expectations. Once you know who *you* are, the path to a happy and healthy relationship is much easier to create.

Rori: This is the world we live in now, where threesomes, adding other people to the mix, and professional sex workers are supposed to be socially acceptable, or even part of committed relationships. Maybe that's your thing, and maybe it's not. Either way, you'd better make damn sure you know what your partner's thing is.

For example, if you're dating a man who expects a threesome every year on his birthday, you need to know about that expectation *before* you commit to him. Some men want to go to a strip club with their buddies. Some people, men and women, feel that they aren't satisfied unless they're getting a little extra excitement on the side. The pool boy. The massage therapist that gives a happy ending. If that's part of your boyfriend's sexuality, know that it's part of the deal. You will not be able to change that desire or lock it down. Don't even try. He *will* get what he wants.

Dr. Gluck: In this case, you can't control what your partner wants, but you can control to what boundaries you commit. If the relationship you're looking for doesn't include other people, and your date needs at least one lap dance a week, that is probably not going to be a match. There are deeper ethical and sociological conversations around sex, of course. Non-monogamy is enjoying a vogue right now. That doesn't mean it needs to be right for you.

Rori: The point is, if it's not right for you, don't do it. Extra people change the dynamic of a relationship, and you deserve to know if you are expected to get down and dirty with additional sexual partners.

Dr. Gluck: Honesty is the best policy.

Rori: Yeah, it is. My other rule is, if he comes home and gives you a sexually transmitted disease, throw him out the window. But before you do, increase his life insurance policy and make sure it's paid up-to-date.

Timing is Everything

Dr. Gluck: In making matches, we talk honestly about sexual preferences, limits, and fantasies. There's also an important element of *time*. Be mindful of time. Be aware about the window of opportunity in the relationship. This is another aspect of relationships that aren't addressed by dating apps. Often, people have trouble acknowledging that they have expectations about time or how the relationship will unfold. Their fear of upsetting their partner turns into an ongoing nightmare that they will have to face at some point in their lives.

Rori: We commonly see *time* being a dealbreaker for women in their mid- to late thirties. They want to have a baby, and that clock is *tick, tick, tick*-ing. The temptation is to date a few guys at once and pick the one who's the most viable. Or, they hurry through dating and marriage so they can settle down to having babies. It can feel counterintuitive to go slowly for women who really have that strong drive to get pregnant and start a family. I get it!

However, there are still boxes you have to check. It's one thing to date and find a partner. If family is what's driving you, make that a priority. But always think through the consequences of going too fast. Speeding into parenthood will bite you in the ass. If you rush to have a baby, you're then increasing the risk of getting divorced down the line. You skipped the "getting to know you" stage, and you end up with a man who—big surprise—you don't know that well! And you want to raise a child with that person! Because you tried to fast-forward your life, you're now dealing with years of finding out that your marriage doesn't work. All the time you thought you were saving, is now wasted on getting divorced, feeling bitter, and putting your child through a difficult situation.

You don't always need a man to raise a child, especially if you have the resources to do it by yourself. In some cases, it's a smarter choice than cutting corners. I respect women who have babies on their own, because it's their choice; they want to be a parent. If having a baby is truly the only thing a woman desires, why bother doing the whole dance around dating, marriage, and the rest of it? If she wants to do that on her own and knows it will make her happy, it's her body. It's way better than ending up with the wrong guy.

Dr. Gluck: Often, we hear people say, "I'm not committed to anyone! Can I date just to date?" You can. But it does end up becoming a process of elimination, either way. At some point, you will have to choose *one*. For Platinum Poire, we don't match more than one person at a time. When you narrow the field, you narrow your focus. You can get intimate and involved. After our recommended three to four dates, you should know whether you can continue, or if you need to find a new person to date.

Rori: Not everyone is confident or self aware enough to just be themselves, right off the bat. That's the only time element with which you should be concerned, early in the process. Let yourself enjoy the moment. Don't worry about doing this "divide and conquer" thing. You'll miss important signals and potential red flags that will screw you over in the long run.

Emotional Monogamy

Dr. Gluck: Just as sexual monogamy is sometimes treated like a relic of the past, so is emotional monogamy. The romance of a meaningful connection is still as powerful as ever. It's in our music, films, media—everywhere. Yet, we don't acknowledge that the power of that connection comes from emotional monogamy. Emotional monogamy is when our romantic intentions are focused on only one person at a time. It's an attachment that forms, with or without sexual reinforcement. It's a bond that can, with time, develop into deep, lasting love.

Rori: Emotional monogamy is where the rubber hits the road in terms of dating without compromise. Decide to whom you become attached. If you're dating for keeps, with the intention of finding a marriage partner, be hyper aware to whom you're giving your time and attention. It can develop into the magic that we call *love*.

Dr. Gluck: Doing things "the old-fashioned way," with kisses, dates, playing together, and conversations, can seem slow at first. We recommend this method for dating because once love begins to blossom, it is very influential.

Many people think of falling in love as something that happens by accident. We know that healthy marriages are created with *intention, respect, and honesty*. With those principles in mind, choose people who reflect your values for a long-term relationship when you date. Sex can affect your judgment and can make you feel attached to someone who's not a great pairing.

Rori: You'll never get sick of hearing me say it: take it slow! The guy who turns you on may not be the one you want to take home to meet your family. This is why we don't encourage the idea that opposites attract. You know the difference between a fun fling with a bad boy, and a date with your future husband. Fun is fun, but you need to keep your future in mind. You need to know yourself. If you know that you're one to become emotionally attached, pull back. I don't want to dull your sparkle, but you need to make sure you're dating someone who can follow through and stand the test of time.

Dr. Gluck: Most people need to be in a monogamous relationship—physically and emotionally monogamous—before they even sleep together. This is why dating multiple people or playing the field doesn't create trust. You need to build intimacy, which means *only* giving your attention to the one person with whom you genuinely want to create a relationship. You don't lose out when you focus on one person at a time. Multitasking, juggling multiple partners or dates, and trying to have it all—or have it all at once—equals operating at 50 percent of your ultimate potential. A worthy partner can sense this, and they might take a pass because they can tell you aren't completely present.

Rori: I want to say a few words about men and commitment. We have this idea that only women want this big love story. Or that only women care about romance and their soulmate. This is *so* not true. Some men care more about emotional monogamy than women do. They're hardwired to commit. They're genuinely looking for Ms. Right, and they're not screwing around. Men are like taxis: when their light is on, it's on! I know plenty of men who were perfectly happy fucking around and didn't care about marriage. There was no changing their minds, no matter how delightful their girlfriends were. The light was off, that's it. But then, all of a sudden, if that light turned on? Watch out! The same man is out shopping for a wife. He's grown up, he's forty, he wants a partner. When that light is on, then he's ready to be emotionally monogamous.

It depends on his intention. I love something Cher says: "Men are a luxury, not a necessity." You could say the same thing about women, right? This is a reality check, because we are often looking for someone to complete us. We forget that the perfect partner is the one who complements who we are and can grow with us. They should add something to your life. Do you *need* them? Over time, yes, you will come to feel you can rely on them. But that's later. In the beginning, remind yourself that searching for your soulmate is no different than selecting a silk tie or a new Bentley. Partnership is a desire, but it is not a necessity. If you come to the table knowing that you're a whole person, and you respect yourself, you'll have a better outcome than someone who's desperate to partner up with the first guy who looks her way.

Dr. Gluck: In matching people, we choose pairs that make sense. We select matches who would be naturally inclined to each other, emotionally, socially, politically, and financially. In your relationships, pick dates who are the kind of people you know make sense for you. For example, two factors that can create irreconcilable conflicts are a serious age mismatch or deep religious convictions. It's possible to overcome these issues, but for most people, they end up being dealbreakers. Repeatedly choosing to attach yourself to partners who are unavailable in some sense, or unworthy of your affection, is something to work out with professional help.

Rori: Emotional monogamy is desirable. The reason we bring it up in relation to sex is that sex can cloud your judgment. You don't need me to tell you that! If you are attracted to someone, your senses are in overdrive. Pause and think about it. Ask yourself, *is this age difference crazy?* Does the other person have kids, and do they want more?

When you're dating, it's so tempting to fall in love too fast. That magic is fun! Romance is a high. Don't lose sight of what you really want because someone cute smiled at you at a party. It's one thing to have fun with someone; if the fun continues, you'll end up attached. Sex can become addicting, and it can be a huge distraction. You may passively end up in a relationship that isn't great for you, or one that doesn't go anywhere.

Kissing is not screwing. But don't kid yourself. When you pucker up, or pop your buttons, ask yourself: *Where is this going? Do I want to go that way?*

Dr. Gluck: When your brain and your body are working in tandem, you have the best likelihood of making integrated decisions based on your values, not your impulses. Every power couple knows this, and they all have one thing in common: they've chosen one another, based on their chemistry, and translated that attraction into meaningful, magnetic marriages. Sex can be a tool of manipulation, for better or for worse. Be on your guard and make sure that the bottom half of you and the top half are in dialogue.

Rori: And they're happy. If someone told me my marriage was good for ten years and then I had to renew and I was happy in the marriage, I would be okay with that. I don't want to be miserable just so I can say that I built a dynasty. C'mon, that's crazy, right? Yet, people do that. They stick around in relationships and marriages, just for the sake of being married. They'll stay, even though they just aren't happy.

Dr. Gluck: Human beings are complicated creatures. Our emotions, our intellects, our needs are only part of the picture. There are so many layers, including our ability to analyze and compartmentalize; to perceive nuances; to integrate our early childhood conditioning in terms of beliefs and attitudes; and our morals and personal causes. These important issues make relationships a difficult terrain to navigate without certain skills.

You need to understand who you are and identify your needs and desires. To find the love you want, you have to be able to define your boundaries and parameters. Sex is part of that. The power of sex is deeply influential. Use sexual attraction to your advantage to select a partner who works with your personality and your preferences, and to eliminate partners who aren't cut out to create a life with you.

Chapter 3

What's Your Favorite Position? Mine is CEO

The main issues in every relationship are romance and finances. In modern relationships, especially for power couples, money and sex go hand in hand. They affect one another. Your portfolio is part of the package.

At Platinum Poire, we treat finances and love as complementary aspects of a relationship. Since our agency matches only elite, executive clients, you'd think that money was a no-brainer. In fact, the opposite is true. Billionaires have the same concerns about finances that everyone else does. Every day people need to be just as conscientious about mixing love and money as the one percent.

In previous generations, people would say things like, "Every problem can be settled between the sheets." They thought everything could be worked out in bed. We know now that just as many problems are settled in the couple's boardroom as their bedroom. As your relationship progresses, it's important to have a clear-cut conversation about your financial situation. If you can't talk about money, you are probably not equipped to talk about other important subjects, like sex, children, family, and religion.

In this chapter, Dr. Gluck and Rori will help you assess your financial wellness. Whether your net worth is four figures, seven, or more, you need to learn how to talk about money with your partner. And you need a partner who's well matched for you *financially* as well as *romantically*.

Give Me Six Inches and Six Figures

Rori: If the financial elements of your life are in balance, then you'll have great sex. There are studies that show more people have sex on payday. You think that's a coincidence? It's not. One of my favorite jokes is, "What's six inches long, two inches thick, and makes a woman scream with happiness?" The answer is, "A one-hundred-dollar bill." Money is sexy, and sexual connection thrives in a stable environment.

It's much easier to attract a stable, long-term partner if you are working, financially self-sufficient, and happy with your profession. On the other hand, if you're having trouble at work, your portfolio just took a hit, or you're anxious about the economy, that will affect your sex life. Anxiety is not attractive. A healthy attitude toward money is.

If you're broke and not working, you have no business looking for love. You should put that energy into finding a job! Try explaining to your date that you're between jobs, or that you recently got laid off. They're going to be wondering, *What does this guy bring to the table? How does he support himself? If we get married or move in, is he going to be able to hold down a job?*

Dr. Gluck: The cultural expectations about financial stability are different for men and women. Men are often the breadwinners. They're supposed to be providers. Women often work in "pink collar" jobs, which are service-oriented. They're also paid less, across the board. A man may be more forgiving of a woman's financial situation, because he's looking for a partner who is a nurturer, not a provider.

Now, those expectations are changing—not dramatically, but they are. Thanks to the women's movement, women are more empowered in the workplace. They have access to jobs, prestige, and wealth that weren't open to them before. There are more women in leadership roles. This is good for women and for men. With that said, women in non-traditional roles may face some obstacles in finding a match.

Rori: That's the truth. You know why? Because some guys aren't comfortable with the idea of their wife wearing the pants. They want to be the one who picks up the check, pays the rent, and provides the security. They want everybody to know they do it, too. Guys like that, no matter how much they make, or how enlightened their views about feminism may be, are not going to be happy in a relationship with a woman who out-earns or out-performs him. He'll end up feeling threatened. He needs to feel like he's the "man" in the relationship and may get jealous or even undermine the relationship or cheat as a way to feel like he has his power back.

This dynamic can be avoided if both people are honest with one another while they're dating. She can say, "I make seven figures, I love my job, and I'm not giving up my company so I can stay home and have babies." And he can say, "I am looking for a wife who has very traditional values and has my dinner waiting when I come home every night." They can be adults and just agree that it's not a fit. They save themselves a decade of horrible arguments, power plays, and trying to change one another. A little honesty goes a long way.

Dr. Gluck: There is no "perfect" relationship, or "right" way to do things. There is just what's right for you. Unhappiness comes from pursuing what other people want, instead of making choices aligned with your needs and desires. It's okay to want a traditional relationship. We don't recommend trying to force those values on someone who wants something very different. Remember, opposites attract—but then they may also want to kill each other.

Rori: Many of our clients at Platinum Poire are super-accomplished, polished, elegant women who run their own companies. They're financially successful. Some are caring for children from a previous marriage. They arrived where they are on their own, and they're making it. Those women need partners who honor and acknowledge the hard work they put in, every day. Most of them will not want to go from being a leader at work, to feeling like a servant at home. A high-achieving woman needs a man who's going to celebrate her wins and won't feel like she needs to hide her success just to stroke his ego.

If a guy says he is intimidated by you, ladies, he's not your man. Success should be a turn-on, not a dirty little secret.

Dr. Gluck: We always say that honesty is the best policy, even when talking about subjects that make people squirm. Money is one of those subjects. Finances are deeply connected to the ego: the individual's sense of self. If a person works as a union welder for forty-five years, that's going to be part of their identity. If they are accustomed to a certain lifestyle, that's an important aspect of who they are as well.

This is why we say that opposites do not make great pairings—at least, not for long.

Rori: Healthy expectations and being realistic is how you end up with a good partner, period. If you're a coat check clerk, don't expect to date a Fortune 500 CEO. If you're a starving student, you probably aren't going to match well with a world-class chef with restaurants in six major cities. That's a romantic comedy, not real life. I don't want to burst your bubble, but long-term, meaningful partnerships of that kind are very rare. Dating is about finding someone who's right for you, for life. That's based on balance, respect, and equality in the partnership. You don't want to be a midnight snack or a little dish of arm candy. You deserve to be the main course.

Goal Diggers and Gold Diggers

Rori: One of the issues we deal with, as an elite matchmaking service, is that we inevitably encounter people who are in it for the money. Usually, this is a young woman searching for a significantly older man. His investments have matured, if you catch my drift.

Dr. Gluck: Sometimes, it's the man doing the searching. for a sugar mommy, or a sugar baby. They want a sugar mommy, a mature, wealthy woman to take care of them financially. Older men might look for a sugar baby, a very young girl to spoil. Sex and sexual attraction are part of the equation in all sugaring relationships.

Rori: Either way, that's not what we do. No sugar! We are on a diet.

Dr. Gluck: We create matches that lead to marriage, not arrangements. A platinum pair is priceless. Gold digging, not so much. We talk more about arrangements like these in Chapter Eleven.

Rori: For example, we had one potential client who specified she was looking for a man who was well off financially. That was her number one criteria. She had no other requirements or preferences: not the guy's height, weight, shoe size, ethnicity, *nothing*. She only cared about how big his bank account was. So we asked, "What does 'well-off' mean to you? A hundred million in the bank?"

"No," she replied.

"Three hundred million?"

"Nope."

"Six hundred million?"

"No. He has to have at *least* a billion," she replied.

I said, "Honey, if a billion dollars is the only thing you care about, you're better off looking for a trust fund baby. A financial portfolio is not going to keep you warm at night."

Dr. Gluck: Obviously, this woman had unhealthy expectations, which were not based on the building blocks of a solid, lasting relationship. We didn't take her on as a client. She wanted an arrangement, not a marriage.

The idea that you can order up your perfect mate is a sure sign of failure in love. For example, if a man comes to us who is in his sixties and wants to date a twenty-five-year-old platinum blonde Barbie Doll, who is 5'9" and a double-D, we won't take him on either. He's not looking for a *partner*. He's looking for a toy. Eventually, your toy will deflate.

Rori: He can look elsewhere! The important thing to remember in any partnership is that you can't enter into the other person's world because you want something that belongs to them. Dating someone because they have money, or social status, or access to a professional world you want to be part of, is not *dating* in the sense that it's building a loving, lasting relationship. Using each other, even if it's mutual, is not *dating*.

Dr. Gluck: That's not to say that sugar daddy-type relationships don't work for some people. They do. However, it's touchy, just like unorthodox sexual arrangements. When there's no chemistry and one partner is in it only for the money, the end result depends on whether both partners know it. Take an eighty-year-old man, who's worth a billion dollars. He's looking for a twenty-year-old sugar baby. He doesn't care whether she likes him, or who she is as a person. He is interested only in her doing what he wants her to do. In exchange for marrying him, she'll thinks she'll inherit half a billion dollars when he dies. Obviously, she forgot about the prenup. If they both agree to this, they don't have a *relationship*. What they have is called a business arrangement.

Again, that arrangement is based on the values of the two people in it. Is it immoral? No. In these scenarios, everyone has an agenda. The younger person is providing what the older person wants and which is agreeable to the younger person. So, both parties get what they want and need. The relationship shouldn't be denigrated just because a person is using money to get something of value to them. As long as both individuals are getting something they value, the relationship is as legitimate as any other.

Rori: You're making it sound like gold digging is a good idea, Dr. G.

Dr. Gluck: I'm saying that it's not good and it's not bad. Morality is subjective.

Rori: Well, you're leaving out the important parts. Arrangements, or sugaring relationships, aren't the same as a marriage. It's a business deal, not a partnership. And just as marriage is not a form of elevated prostitution, sugaring is not an alternative form of marriage. They might both involve sharing resources or doing a little give-and-take in the bedroom. But that's where the similarities end.

What the gold digger doesn't realize is that every one of those money-based relationships have an expiration date. I won't even get into the stuff about prenups, or the lengths wealthy men go to protect their assets from their wives and girlfriends. It's so naive to think, *Yeah, all I have to do is marry a billionaire and then all my problems will go away.* I don't think so!

Sex work *is* work. Relationships *take* work. A healthy marriage is an investment that gives back. Coming to marriage with a last-resort mindset is the perfect way to keep anything meaningful from developing between you and the other person. Nobody is going to fix all your problems, financial or otherwise.

Seriously, no judgment on people who want to sugar. I'm just saying, it's a transaction. It's not dating. It's not marriage. It's business. That's why I encourage women to quit focusing on marrying a man with money and *make their own*. Be a *goal* digger, not a gold digger. If a woman comes to the table with nothing of her own, no self worth, no sense of her own value, guess what? She's going to have a hard time finding a man who treats her like she's worthy.

Dr. Gluck: The appeal of those relationships is understandable. To some degree, it's no different than a dating app. You can order what you want, so to speak. You can have an interaction that mimics a relationship, on your terms, with someone who's not really part of your life. As the client, you get to have more control than you might otherwise. However, there's a reason it's called "sugar daddy." These arrangements are emotional junk food. They're no substitute for a real relationship.

Rori: Basically, if you marry a guy for his money, don't be surprised if he treats you like an employee instead of an equal. And I'll tell you another thing. People who want something meaningful, who are dating with intention, are going to see right through the gold digging. They will not buy your act. This is not a *Pretty Woman* kind of setup. You're not going to attract Richard Gere, but you might end up with a guy who looks like Hugh Hefner.

For the Love of Money

Dr. Gluck: Marriage and money have always gone hand in hand. Actually, love is new to the game. Until very recently in human history, probably within the last two centuries, marriage has been treated just like that: a business deal.

59

Marriage united the tribe and the family. Marriage strengthened and expanded the nation by bringing in other tribes and families. Young people, under the age of consent, did what their families wanted them to do or what their parents asked them to do. They got married, set up a household, and had children. Marriage for love is a rather new concept, culturally. I would say that it has not yet been proven to work.

Rori: Hold on. What do you mean "proven to work"?

Dr. Gluck: Well, from a cultural perspective, radical individualism is about three hundred years old. We see it primarily in the West, and the U.S. is known as a country of radical individualism. The result of this unproven theory that marriage should be for love is untold pain and suffering of those who are unhappily married and, within the last twenty years, a surge in divorce. The opposite of love as the basis for marriage is that a lack of love is the basis for divorce.

Rori: Come on, you can't blame lack of love as the sole reason marriages fail. About a million other things happened between men and women in the last two hundred years.

Dr. Gluck: Well, that's true. Historically, people whose marriages were connected to their tribes and families tended to stay married, but they weren't necessarily happier. I think people are happier now. These days, people trade safety for the adventure of love and they do it despite of the fact that the relationship will most likely crash and burn. But it doesn't have to end that way. If you continually reinvent yourself and have tremendous support and patience with your partner, then you're on the way to a successful partnership.

Rori: I agree that the success of a relationship definitely depends on what you start with. Those values, family connections, and what you bring to the table all influence how long a marriage lasts. And a long relationship is not necessarily a happy one. Just because you're married to someone for forty-five years doesn't mean you're happy. I think the secret is to get smart about who you match with: if you don't pick someone who's going to make you miserable, you'll stick around longer, right?

I believe there is such a thing as a soulmate. I feel you are meant to be with a certain kind of person, even if it's not forever, even if it's just for ten years of your life. You needed that person during that time in your life, which was what empowered you then. It's why we have all different kinds of people who come and go from our lives. You don't need to hold onto anyone except that person who's the *right* one.

Dr. Gluck: If you're getting into dating with the mindset that you should just "take what you can get," that's not a healthy place to start. If it's important for you to have a partner who always picks up the check, put that on your list of important qualities. Or, you might be looking for a guy who has a flexible schedule, so he can go to your foundation banquets and fundraising events.

Remember that the average person spends a third of their life at work, and a third of their life asleep. The bonds they form with coworkers are close and can feel like family for some people. Conferences, conventions, and after-hours socializing is very important in some industries. It can even be mandatory.

Rori: Before you commit to someone, you will need to make sure that they're not already married to their work. Do you want to marry a guy who's always looking at his watch, or has to calendar every date weeks in advance? Some people can handle that in the early parts of dating. It can be a dealbreaker later. What works for one person doesn't work for another. Some people like having a partner who's not around all the time! Once you learn what you're working with, you have a decision to make. You either pass and look for someone who has more time for you, or accept that you'll always be second.

Here are some questions that will help you identify your assets when it comes to money:

> For me, money is _____.
> I like having _____ amount of money in my bank account.
> For work to be enjoyable, I must have _____.
> Am I comfortable with budgeting? Do I stick to my budget?
> Do I like my job? Why or why not?
> What are my expectations about my income?
> Am I comfortable talking about money with my partner? Why or why not?
> For me, success is _____.
> Financially, my ideal partner is _____.

> ➤ Do I consider myself good with money? Do I ever ask for help? Would I or have I ever received outside financial support? Why?

> ➤ What's the worst job I've ever had? The best? Why?

> ➤ If I didn't need the money, what kind of work would I do?

> ➤ Where do I see myself in two years, financially? Five? Twenty?

> ➤ What is the most important aspect of money for me?

Dr. Gluck: Financial intelligence isn't something a dating app's algorithm will ask you about. It is a factor that is like chemistry, that can either enhance or diminish your sexual compatibility. It takes time and trust to talk about these subjects and experience what the other person is really like with money.

Money can come to represent different values in your life. How you spend money, what you consider a priority, whether you save or splurge, and how you make financial plans are all keys to understanding who you are. It's important to find someone who matches with you financially. If you are faithfully putting your money into a savings account or an IRA, maxing out your 401K contributions, and you have a penny jar in the kitchen, your ideal match is not someone who's got a dozen credit cards and lives paycheck-to-paycheck.

Rori: The goal is always harmony. In a platinum pair, you enrich one another's lives—in more ways than one.

Dr. Gluck: Now, you may be thinking to yourself, *I'm not a millionaire. I'm not even a thousand-aire! How do I date without feeling insecure about my finances?*

Rori: People are way more squirrelly about money than sex. You can see a table of women dishing at lunch. One is talking about how big her last guy's dick was, just getting raunchy, laughing, and having fun. Every little detail is shared. But if the subject turns to money, the fun is over. Total silence. The same women who were bragging about their conquests one minute ago are completely inhibited about finances. They're funny about money!

It's not that they don't have money—they do. But they've probably been brought up not to talk about it, or at least not to talk about it explicitly. What they don't know is that open, frank conversations about money is just as important as the ones you have about sex.

Dr. Gluck: Many of the clients I work with feel insecure about their finances, no matter how much or how little they have. Their finances are linked to deeper issues of self-esteem, family, and self-confidence. As always, if you feel that you have workaholic tendencies, or if you struggle to talk about money, you will need to seek help to work through those issues. One recurring pattern that I see in many people, whether they are my clients or not, is a fear of scarcity. They fear that they will never have enough, because they don't know what "enough" means.

Rori: They would know what it means if people talked about money!

Rather than feel insecure about your financial situation, focus on your assets. If money is problematic for you, you can also talk to a financial planner at your bank or credit union, educate yourself about money, and commit to a monthly budget. Learn how to improve your credit score. These are issues that can be fixed. If you're really hard up, you can get good financial guidance from a library book or online, for free. You don't necessarily need to become a billionaire by the end of the month, but you should feel confident talking about money, and comfortable with yourself, financially.

Getting your financial health on track is no different than losing weight or committing to go to the gym. If you know that your finances are a problem, and a potential barrier to finding a match, fix them. Put in the effort. It's just like if you gained a bunch of weight. If you don't feel attractive, do something about it. Deal with the things that make you feel insecure, and you'll have less insecurity.

You Show Me Your Portfolio, and I'll Show You Mine

Dr. Gluck: Talking about money is a litmus test for so many other relationship issues. Here are some parameters:

> If you like the person but don't see eye to eye on finances, then there is not enough upon which to build a relationship. You are building on sand, not concrete.

> Not all values need to be agreed upon, but there needs to be a discussion to know which are important to you as a couple.

> An agreement about financial goals must be reached. Do you want to buy a house, a

boat, or a business? Would you accomplish those goals separately or together, and how?

➤ A discussion about how financial decisions are made is important. Who will pay for what? How will you settle financial conflicts?

Rori: When you move forward to a certain point in dating, full financial disclosure is necessary. Each partner needs to discuss where he or she is now. When you have this conversation, you need to keep an understanding that each person's situation can change over time. Like I said, credit can be repaired. People get promotions. They change careers. Nothing is set in stone, but the important thing is, did you talk about it?

Also, how did the conversation go? If you tried to bring up money and were shot down or didn't feel comfortable enough to really get down to dollars and cents, pay attention to those signals. Listening and communication are skills that must be learned, respected, and executed in order to have a successful relationship. If you can't talk about money, what can you talk about?

Dr. Gluck: Talking about money is as important as the discussions you'll share regarding each other's abilities and beliefs about sex, politics, and spiritual life. *Not* talking about those things creates an opening for terrible conflict and misunderstandings.

Rori: At any point, you can check in with yourself and make sure that you're dating someone who really matches your values. You deserve to have what you desire. Think about how your ideal match will fit into your life, financially. Do they make more than you? Less? Do they have a trust fund, or are they self-made? Is their job just a job, or part of their personality? Do they work twenty hours a week, forty hours, or around the clock? You have to consider all these things when you're picking your partner for life.

You're allowed to have preferences. Remember, you should be looking to commit *without compromise.* Fortunes can change, but people rarely do.

Chapter 4

The Art of Flirting

Variety is the spice of life. Flirting is a way to get a little taste of everything. When you flirt, you explore the chemistry you share with another person. Flirting expresses your natural sexiness and your interest in other people. Sometimes, it leads to a meaningful connection—and sometimes, it's just for fun!

Flirting is a communication style that tells the world, *I'm here, I like myself, and you might like me too.* It takes confidence to flirt. This type of light, sexy conversation is fun. It's usually light but can leave both people tingling. On a date, flirting keeps the words flowing. If conversation is a fine wine, flirting is champagne. It has that extra sparkle that makes you feel special, appreciated, and attractive. Everyone has their own distinct flirting style, which makes flirting exciting and new with every person. Whether you're flirting with your boyfriend, your friend's new baby, or your barista, you'll experience a little thrill.

When you're reentering the dating game, looking for a new match, or you want to let others know you're available and eager to mingle, flirting is a *must*. You can use it as a social tool, signaling that you're open to making new connections. The right kind of flirting can get you a phone number, or even a date. It can also be a turn-off if it's done the wrong way! In this chapter, Rori and Dr. Gluck will share how flirting works, how to talk to people in a way that makes them feel good, and how flirting can boost your self esteem.

Share That Sexy Energy

Dr. Gluck: When two people who both have high sexual energy get together, it creates a sexual energy that is attention-grabbing. That sexual energy is significantly higher on the priority list than other items. It demands attention. It creates a playfulness, a back-and-forth banter that is fun for both people. Flirting comes from a need for an emotional connection and a desire to continue connecting to the person you are with. In flirting, there is a continual desire to be close and intimate, to touch and be touched.

You can touch someone with your words, your eyes, or your gestures. As a forensic profiler, I know how powerful a look or a simple movement can be. It reveals so much about the person. For example, giving someone "bedroom eyes" conveys an unmistakable message: *I want to see more of you.* Touching someone's arm or adjusting their necktie is exciting because it's intimate. People with tons of personal chemistry are usually flirting and putting out those signals all the time, even when there's no individual recipient of the flirting. They're flirting with the universe.

Rori: Sexiness is contagious. It's the only sexually transmitted thing worth catching! When you're feeling sexy, attractive, and good about yourself, that naturally flows out of you. If you have one of those mornings where you're just feeling it, you flirt with everyone. You flirt with your reflection. You flirt with your husband. You flirt with your coworkers. Flirtiness says, *I've got it, so come get it.*

Even people who do not have an insane amount of chemistry can become incredibly attractive when they flirt. It's all about the delivery. Suddenly, the person who wasn't the best-looking person in the room, the richest, or the youngest is the most magnetic. You can't look away from them. And when they talk to you, you feel good. You're making a connection, and that's sexy.

Dr. Gluck: Birds do their mating dance: humans flirt. It's one of the ways that people demonstrate their sexuality. Of course, flirting is very culturally specific, even within subcultures. An American man flirts very differently from a French one. An American man *from Brooklyn* flirts differently from a guy who was born and raised in Des Moines. The style is individual and influenced by the cultural values in which the person grew up. Gay and straight cultures flirt differently, and so do people of different generations. Although sexual magnetism is undeniable, flirting sends a specific signal that will be especially attractive to people of your same cultural background. From your personal grooming to the way you touch someone, your flirting says something about *you.*

Rori: We've all been there: we see a good-looking person, feel attracted, flirt them up a little bit, and then walk away feeling like it all fell flat. The flirting didn't work. Maybe they didn't respond how you wanted, or even acknowledge your flirting. What happened? Did you have spinach in your teeth? Garlic breath?

Well, it might not be you. It's possible that you weren't giving off signals that the other person could read.

You're on FM and they're on AM. The move you thought was flirty didn't register for them. Try not to take it personally. Move on and flirt with someone else, who can pick up what you're putting down.

Flirting, like any other skill, gets better with practice. Some people—especially those bad boys we love so much, who make us crazy—are almost *too* good at it. An experienced player has those flirting skills that are irresistible and will keep you coming back for more even when you know it's not great for you. He knows how to touch you, how to talk to you, how to make you feel special. He will also break your heart because he's doing the same thing with six other women, and sleeping with them, too. The good news is, great guys who are looking to commit can learn those moves too. The difference is, the player is flirting and making empty promises. The guy you want to date and eventually marry can make good on every word he says.

Dr. Gluck: There's a cultural narrative that reliable guys, who are husband material, do not have the ability to flirt. Men who are good fathers, great partners, and responsible employees are portrayed as awkward, stuffy, and even goofy. They tell "dad jokes." They wear out-of-date clothes that don't flirt with the eye. These stereotypes say that mature men have an old-school flirting style that stopped working in 1979—around the time they got out of college. Nothing could be farther from the truth.

Rori: Just like your hairstyle, tailoring, and cologne, flirting is a verbal sign that you have chemistry. It's a form of advertising. You look nice, you smell nice, and you talk nice, too. Right? If you're looking your best, you need to sound your best as well. Don't put in the work of overhauling yourself and then miss out because you were afraid to be flirty. You have a lot to offer, and flirting alerts likely partners that you're on the lookout for someone with whom to play.

Flirting is a skill that can be learned. How many CEOs have I met who are learning Japanese so they can excel in their business meetings? So many! They'll put in hours of practice, learning how to order in restaurants, how to impress others in the boardroom, how to give a presentation—all in a foreign language. But you ask them about flirting? Most of them couldn't flirt their way out of a Saturday afternoon at Sephora. They'll do billion-dollar deals in Japanese, but they get scared to flirt because it seems like the stakes are too high. How does *that* make sense?

Dr. Gluck: Flirting can feel high-pressure if you're new to dating or recovering from a divorce. We get it. Those experiences can make you feel like every word either makes or breaks the situation. You flirt, say the wrong thing, and bam! The spell is broken. The other person walks away, making you feel like a schmuck.

Flirting should not make you feel disappointed. It's sexy, playful. That's why keeping things light and positive is important, especially if you're just starting out. A simple compliment counts as flirting, or a smile. Practice with the little things, until you feel confident enough to try more. Your comfort zone will grow as you become more at-ease with yourself and your skills.

Rori: I flirt all the time. It makes me feel good, and it makes other people feel good, too. I like the attention! I like people to know that I see them and appreciate them. And my flirting, which is always based on being friendly, doesn't cross any lines. It could be as simple as touching my hair when I'm talking to someone who I think is hot or holding eye contact with them just a split second longer than usual. It gives me a little buzz. Now, I'm not going to go any farther than that—thanks, I'm happily married! But my sense of being sexy and desirable affects my marriage in a positive way. I feel sexy, and that is very attractive for my husband.

Putting on Your Fuck-Me Heels

Rori: As we discussed in the first chapter, attraction starts with the eyes. You see someone and *hello*, you notice them. They capture your attention. Their physical self is attractive to the eye. You noticed his shoes, his watch, and his package, and it's working for you! Or you caught a glimpse of her bare shoulder or the way her legs look in those Louboutins and your head snaps around on your neck. Wow! Instant chemistry.

Your outfit is a visual way of flirting with others. Women know this, and we know how to turn it way up. Remember, fashion is foreplay! Flirting is, too. Dressing a certain way, a little more over-the-top than usual, is very flirty.

For men, this means incorporating a pop of color in your necktie or pocket square. Keep your sock pattern neutral, unless you're trying to attract other men. You might also add an interesting fabric, like a Kiton blazer or a cashmere sweater. You can select fabrics that have an appealing texture. They send the message, *touch me*. Also,

73

nothing is sexier than a woman stroking your arm or shoulder and purring, "Is this cashmere?" It gives her an excuse to touch you, which opens the door for more flirting.

Women know how to get that sexual attention. It's not hard, right? Cleavage up to *here*, legs for days, high heels, tousled hair, and distinctive makeup all send the message that you want to be noticed. Now, the female body is inherently sexy. A sensual perfume, body-hugging dress, and earrings that draw attention to your face and neck are class-sexy ways of flirting with the eye. Diamonds are great for this, because they glitter, catching the light and showing off your natural sparkle. A bright, white smile and sparkling, white diamonds are a classy-sexy combination!

To send a flirty message, you don't need to show your boobs to everyone, or dress inappropriately. Above all, confidence is key: nothing is worse than seeing a woman who's trying too hard, way overdressed and wearing too much makeup, teetering around in her fuck-me heels—and looking totally miserable. If you're going to dress super-sexy, make sure you feel comfortable with yourself. Also, don't let your clothes overshadow your personality and charm. If a guy is just staring down your dress all night, there's no way he's listening to the words you're saying. Flirting is about balance, the dance between two people. Your style should complement you.

Dr. Gluck: People are visual. That's true for both women and men. At its core, flirting is a way of acknowledging and appreciating a detail about someone that caught your eye. If your date looks especially attractive—maybe she's wearing a pretty scarf or red lipstick—you can mention that. Your compliment shows that you noticed the effort she took to dress up, and that you appreciate being in her presence.

Flirting should always be polite and respectful, just like any other form of communication. That means no grabbing, slapping, spanking, pinching, or mean teasing. You are not a kid on the playground, so don't pull anyone's pigtails. The best flirting is completely appropriate for mixed company and doesn't compromise your partner's boundaries. You could do it in front of your family and not ruffle any feathers. Face-to-face flirting is exciting in part *because* others can see you doing it. The sexual energy you share with the other person is compelling and exciting. You can create tension without laying a finger on one another or saying anything you couldn't say at your family's dinner table. It's *how* you communicate, not *what*.

Think about classic movie stars, like Lauren Bacall or Humphrey Bogart. They were perfectly proper with one another, but their sexual energy spoke volumes. Bacall could order a martini in a voice that would set your hair on fire, it was so charged. On the one hand, it's just a martini. On the other, it was extremely sexy, flirtatious communication.

Rori: Classic is definitely classy-sexy. I think of George Clooney: he's like a Chanel suit. Classiness goes both ways, whether you're the person flirting or the one being flirted with. Remember, just because someone is flirting with you, or because they're dressed to the nines, doesn't mean they're asking to be groped. Follow your partner's cues, and you'll find it easy to read whether they want to keep flirting, or if they're ready to move on.

Men, respect is a *huge* turn-on for women. That means, don't grab her ass to let her know you're into her. Don't compliment her new implants unless she asks you to check them out. Look into her eyes when she speaks and let her know you're really listening.

Flirting isn't just the way you say hello, it's how you leave the room, too. Disengaging gracefully can be very sexy. Saying goodbye like a gentleman to a woman you've flirted with can end up being the move that truly captures her interest. You know what they say: "I hate to see you go, but I love to watch you walk away!" Flirting is exciting because it builds anticipation for the next time. You leave the other person wanting more, wondering when they'll see you again. That's the fun of it, for both of you!

Slow Burn, or Jack Rabbit Style?

Dr. Gluck: Let's go back to Bogart and Bacall. They didn't just sizzle: they smoldered. Their flirting style was a slow burn. It intensified over an hour or more, one conversation at a time. Audiences loved their double entendres, the building tension, and their chemistry that set the screen on fire. That mode of sexual expression is now considered old-fashioned, because it's deliberate. Slow-moving. It takes time to build. Patience is not popular in the modern dating world, but there's no doubt that rushing through the fun parts of dating is not very smart—or enjoyable.

Rori: Whenever someone tells me, "I'm so over dating. It's boring, it takes too much time, and every person I go out with is the same!" I immediately know that they're a jack rabbit. Nothing will be fast enough for them. They want to power through dating, hurry up and find their perfect match, and then settle down immediately. *Bang, bang, bang,* and then they're married! Just like a little bunny.

People who go through dating like jack rabbits end up learning the hard way that you can't rush quality. Slowing down not only shows you what you're really working with in a relationship. It is also pleasurable. If you're not excited to go on a date, why are you even dating? Are you going out with people because you think you "should" have plans for a Saturday night? Or did you agree to have dinner because that person flirted with you, made you feel attractive, and then asked if you'd join them at a table for two?

Those are two very different scenarios, right? Flirting is fun. That's why people do it. Yes, dating can be discouraging, but if you're truly paying attention to the sexy signals someone's putting out, you'll get a good idea of who is going to dazzle you—and who is going to disappoint.

Dr. Gluck: It's said that chivalry is dead. That may be true, but communication isn't. We no longer live in an era where, if you want to capture a lady's attention, you have to slay a dragon or cut someone's head off. Thank goodness! Men and women have both adapted to communicating their desires differently. Much of that is transmitted when we flirt. However, I question whether we should bring back a dragon or two, just to slow some people down.

Although communication between the sexes is at an all-time high, the quality of that communication is somewhat degraded by the speed and ease of how it happens. Just think, in the olden days, you had to borrow a horse, ride to the next town, bargain with your beloved's father, and offer her family a gift just to spend an hour in her presence. A supervised hour, with a chaperone! Try flirting under those conditions. Things have significantly changed, just in the last century.

When I was a young man in the 1960s, we'd partially dispensed with the formalities of our great-grandparents' generation, but there was still a time element. We had different etiquette, too. You would have to call a girl at home if you wanted to talk to her or hope to meet her at a club or a dance. We sent letters in the mail to our sweethearts. I remember riding the subway all the way across town, or catching a bus, in the name of love. If we wanted to flirt with someone, or ask them on a date, we needed to proceed slowly. Girls lived at home longer and were usually with their friends when they went out. There was usually a chaperone or a friend who came along. There was no internet dating then, because there was no internet.

Rori: And now, we are supposed to fall in love after *one* text message. People use dating apps to order themselves a soulmate, like love is Chinese delivery. They buy into the idea that dating, like Amazon Prime, is something you can get with one click. But real love, and real relationships, don't follow the rules. They're not predictable. You can set the stage for love, you can prepare for it, and you can make sure that you're your best self. You can be ready and willing. But love happens on its own schedule, in its own way. That's what makes every love story special.

The things Dr. G describes, like with the horse and the love letters—that sounds romantic to me. Inconvenient, sure, but so what? With love, there is no imposition. A guy who can't handle a little inconvenience is not going to be okay dealing with real life. I also think that old-fashioned manners are attractive, up to a point. Now, you see *everything* before you even meet the person. It's crazy! It kills the mystery.

Seriously, is it romantic to say, "Yeah, he sent me a dick pic on Tinder, so we met up to Netflix and chill. We fucked for a month while we were both casually seeing other people, and then his lease was up and he lost his job so he I let him move in, and that's how I knew he was the one?" Do you want to tell your grandkids that story? Do you want to share it with all of your friends and family at your wedding? No, it's not romantic at *all*. It's actually kind of depressing. Yet, people do this, thinking they'll end up with a fairy tale ending.

At Platinum Poire, we understand that people— men and women both, even if they're pressed for time— want romance. No matter what you've been through, you still deserve a love story. Romance happens when you take it slow, savoring every minute together. It's not the click-and-swipe instant gratification of a hookup or an anonymous first date. It's not dick-pics and nudes from strangers. It's the process of getting to know each other, flirting, and feeling each other out. It's the slow mornings in bed. Lingering over dessert. Long walks by the water, holding hands and making each other laugh. Slow kisses. Slow dancing. What do these things have in common? They're *slow*. If it's a fit, you won't want the moment to end.

Dr. Gluck: The opposite of fast isn't slow, it's intentional. We always encourage people to take their time.

Selecting the person you date, with the idea of eventually marrying, is a big decision. You don't rush things like that. Those choices should not be made impulsively. It may be exciting to jump in head-first, without looking or thinking, but the outcome is rarely good. And our culture is experiencing "romance burn-out," thanks to apps and dating sites that encourage speedy matching. It's possible to experience romance fatigue, if you've tried to date multiple people in a short period or fallen down a dating rabbit hole.

We suggest *one* date a time, for this reason. Flirting face-to-face enables you to observe and enjoy the other person's company.

When You're Dancing Cheek-to-Cheek

Dr. Gluck: When I profile someone, I sit across from them in a relaxed setting. Usually, we meet in my office, where I have a few comfortable chairs set up, soft lighting, and lots of privacy. It's not a *romantic* place—obviously, I work there—but it's *intimate*. It encourages people to open up. At the beginning of the session, I look into the other person's eyes, smile at them, and observe them while they speak. Now, I'm not flirting with them. But I am noticing that when I say something kind or complimentary, they respond.

It's the same in the dating game. When you look into someone's eyes, they *have* to notice you. The eyes make the first connection.

Rori: The eyes are the windows to the soul. One tried-and-true, old school method of flirting is simply to make eye contact. There is something primal about looking into someone's eyes. If two sexy people are looking at each other across the room, that's exciting. A glance or two in the which you make eye contact—for three seconds, max!—paired with a subtle smile, sends the message that you're interested. You want to learn more.

Dr. Gluck: Eye contact creates an opportunity for conversation. Let's say that you cast a few glances at the person you want to meet, and smile. They smile back. Then, they start to come over to you. What then? What do you say?

Rori: Whatever you do, don't panic! This is what you wanted, to draw them closer. As they walk up, take a look at them. Are they as attractive up close as they were from across the room? What do they smell like? Do they trip on their feet or are they graceful and confident?

Then, once you've said hello, give them a compliment. You can't go wrong with an earnest compliment. Look for something about them that you find flattering—their cocktail of choice, their outfit—and comment on it in a positive way. If they've put some effort into their appearance, compliment them. If you're not sure exactly what to say, it's alright to keep it general. "You look stunning," is acceptable, as is "What are you drinking tonight?" It helps break the ice and let the other person know that you are interested in talking with them.

Another nice compliment is to mention something you saw the person do, like give up their seat to another person, or help get the waiter's attention.

Dr. Gluck: If your compliment is insincere, it will sound like you're giving the person a line. You can avoid by noticing the things that make them distinctive, individual. It's okay to say, "You have beautiful eyes," but if the woman hears that all the time—let's say she has exceptionally beautiful eyes and is wearing makeup that accentuates them—your compliment might sound insincere. It won't make her feel special. Choose a compliment that might surprise or please the other person and give them a clue that you notice things about them that other people don't.

Rori: On the flip side, if you *get* a compliment that isn't blowing your mind, but the person is still super attractive, throw them a bone. You can give the person a break by not giving a cynical response. It would be easy to say, "I bet you tell that to all the girls," which is pretty much guaranteed to nip the flirtation in the bud. Nothing kills flirtation like sarcasm: it's rude and deflating. Instead, politely say, "Thank you." Give the person credit for trying. Move the conversation along or give them a compliment in return. Don't let them twist around and get all awkward. C'mon, they're trying here! They took the risk to come over, and that takes courage.

Dr. Gluck: When you flirt, consider the nonverbal cues you're giving as well. Gestures speak louder than words. When you're not interested in someone, you lean back, turn away, cross your arms, or get busy with your phone. When you want to show that you're listening and engaged, uncross your arms. Make eye contact when you speak, put your phone away, and casually tuck your hair behind your ear.

Rori: How would you do that? You don't have any hair!

Dr. Gluck: I don't need hair to show a lady that I'm interested! Body language speaks volumes. When I met my wife, she was walking down the street in the Village, and I went right up to her and asked her to lunch. She was out doing some shopping. I really turned on the charm. She thought I was crazy! She said, "No way, get out of here!" But I convinced her to walk with me, and we got to know each other. That spontaneous lunch turned into much more. Our relationship started with that initial attraction, though—the eye contact, the look, the flirtation.

Rori: Point taken. The hair is optional, the eye contact is not!

Flirting Without Fucking Up

Rori: Flirting is not the same as being slutty. Just as kissing is not screwing, flirting is not fucking. Flirting can lead to the bedroom, but it's not a guarantee that you'll end up with anything except a nice endorphin rush. When you flirt, keep in mind that you don't have to make it physical. You also don't have to do more than hint about your attraction to the other person. Attraction can just be *attraction*.

If you want to be courted, keep that in mind when you flirt. It's okay to hold back a little bit. Part of the excitement of flirting is that you *don't* see it all. You tease. You play. You bite your lip. You don't sit on the guy's lap within five minutes of meeting him.

Dr. Gluck: Flirting should make you feel good, not guilty. When you flirt, respect your own boundaries and keep your goal in mind. Are you flirting to have fun, or are you on the hunt? At the end of the day, flirting is a mutual massage for the ego. Each person gets to feel sexy, attractive, and interesting. You should both walk away feeling good about yourself, not compromised. If you're thinking about the interaction later and feeling like maybe you overdid it, well—that's probably because you did.

Rori: As I said, I'm married, and my marriage is sacred to me. I know who I am, and I know what my home and my husband mean to me. I can flirt and be very fun and sexy, but I would never do anything to embarrass myself or my husband. There's a difference between fun, social flirting and the words and actions that might make people wonder if I have an ulterior motive. It's all about intention.

If you act desperate, and you take flirting too far, you'll end up disappointed or making a fool of yourself. The right amount of flirting says, "I wanna dance with somebody." The wrong amount, where you take it over the line, says, "I don't respect myself and neither should you."

Dr. Gluck: If you're a person who is recently out of a serious relationship, you may not have those clearly defined limits. Or you may feel stiff and uncomfortable, like you're trying to make small talk. As Rori said, your *motive* in flirting is what's important. Are you flirting because it's pleasurable and you like feeling good? That will shine through in the way you communicate. Are you flirting because you're scared of being alone, or insecure? Are you seeking attention because you need validation in order to feel whole? Those are issues that will also be apparent. Those signals will attract the wrong people and repel the right ones. Check your motive, and you can change your flirting style accordingly.

Rori: Flirting is *flirting*. Some people take it so seriously! But it's not meant to be that way. A flirtation is not a promise, it's not a long-term relationship. It's a sweet treat, a little pick-me-up for your day. Keep it light, and you'll have fun.

Chapter 5

From the First Audition to the Final Ovation

When you are ready to do more than rub noses and flirt with good-looking strangers, it's time to take things to the next level. That means planning a fun, romantic date. The first date is the audition. It reveals more about each person: how they behave when you're one-on-one together, whether they're easy to talk to and fun to be with, and whether you'd like to see them again. If the first date goes well, the odds are good that you'll see each other again. So how do you make that first date a night to remember?

When you make plans with a new person, it can feel like a high-pressure situation. Especially for younger people, the temptation might be to dial it down, stick with group dates, or do something low-key instead of turning up the heat. If you do this, you're missing an opportunity to really show your date your assets. If you're dating with the intention of becoming exclusive with someone, you need to know how much you enjoy their company. Life is long, and in every marriage, you spend a tremendous amount of time together! Don't cut corners on your first date—or any date.

When your date goes well, you can move forward with building a relationship. You develop the beginnings of an intimate connection with the person. The butterflies you felt when you flirted with them turns into something more. So, what actually happens on a good date? How do you know if the person is truly compatible with you, worth your time, and a potential match? When does a date become *dating*?

This chapter explores the three distinct stages of dating: the first time you meet, agreeing to be exclusive, and setting a wedding date. Rori and Dr. Gluck provide support and insight on how to transition seamlessly from one stage to the next, without losing your sense of self *or* compromising your relationship goals.

Saturday Night Fever

Rori: Your first date with someone is exciting! Finally, you have the chance to see how they make that first official impression. You may have chatted them up at Starbucks or traded sexy smiles for a few weeks—and now, after exchanging numbers, they've agreed to go out with you this Saturday night. On a *real* date. That's the big leagues.

Now, my idea of a real date is pretty straightforward. I can tell you what it's *not*. It's not casual. It's not a hangout session. It's not a group date. And it's not something you could or would do every day. Catch my drift? If you see a gorgeous woman and you ask her out, half-assing the first date is a great way to give her the signal that she shouldn't take your interest seriously. Come on! She's a knockout. If you want to get to know her better, don't take her to an arcade to play laser tag with ten of your buddies from work. No. You find a romantic spot with a good wine list and soft lighting.

Dr. Gluck: Traditionally, the man is the one who does the asking when it comes to planning the first date. This is changing: women now feel more empowered to invite men to dinner. However, that's still the exception, not the rule. A woman may give strong signals that she's interested, and still not make the initial offer to get together. Men, do not lean on women's liberation when it comes to romance. Even the most independent, self-sufficient, successful woman—a woman who's a CEO, a leader in every other aspect of her life—likes to be asked on a date. Those traditional gender roles are still in place and should be honored.

Rori: We like our men to be *men*. It's attractive when a man is comfortable initiating a date, holding the door, pulling out the chair at dinner, picking up the check. It shows respect, that he'll treat you like a lady. So guys, if you want a date, you've gotta ask. Don't bat your eyelashes and play shy. The odds are good that the girl on whom you're focusing is feeling the same way. One of you has to make the first move, and guess what? That's *you*.

Dr. Gluck: The jitters that come with putting yourself out there are natural. Having a plan in mind can give you more confidence. When you ask someone on a date, offer a day and an activity. That forestalls the awkward conversation, "So what do you want to do?" It's better to invite your date out by saying something like, "I'd love to take you to dinner on Saturday. Are you available?" That shows your date that you're not wasting her time. You've got a game plan. It also gives her the opportunity to gracefully decline or extend a counteroffer.

Let's say that you love the movies, but she'd much rather spend the evening getting to know you. She doesn't want to sit in a dark theater for two hours, in silence, eating popcorn. If you ask her to see a movie, she can say, "Sure, let's have dinner first!" She might also tell you that she prefers a poetry reading or something more intimate. The counteroffer is not a sign that you've made the wrong move. It tells you that she is interested in *you*, not a movie.

Rori: You can pull all the stops out on the first date. Pick a restaurant where you'll have some privacy, and where you're comfortable with the menu and the service. You may be an adventurous eater and want to check out a new place. Save that for a second or third date option: for the first date, you want to have as much control as possible over the setting. A bad entree or sloppy waiter can ruin the romantic atmosphere you're trying so hard to create. A dinner date in a place you frequent and can even recommend your favorite dish from the menu, is a nice touch. It will make her feel like she's entering your world a little bit. She'll get to learn more about you.

Obviously, if she's a vegetarian, don't take her to a steakhouse! By the time you ask her to dinner, you should have figured out a few things about her preferences. Maybe she spent some time traveling in China and loves Sichuan cuisine. Maybe she went to culinary school and knows a few things about French food! You can impress her by mentioning the reason you're picking a particular restaurant: "You said you loved your trip to Cannes last month. There's a wonderful place on the Upper East Side that does a traditional Provencal dinner menu. I'd love to take you there on Saturday, if you're available." That sure beats a hot dog and a walk in the park!

Dr. Gluck: For most people, simply asking for a date is the biggest hurdle. You can't get the prize until you ring the bell.

Rori: Yes, the planning of a date is another good mini-test for how you work together as a couple. Maybe you can agree on the time and place, no problem. That's easy. But with two adults, who work and might have kids at home, it's a little more complex. The date that was going to be this Saturday is suddenly three weeks away, because one of your kids has a soccer tournament that night, or one of you has a business trip and will be out of town over the weekend. To those situations, I say: are you sure you have time to date? However, if you can choose a day, place, and time that works for *both* of you, you've shown that you can be flexible and negotiate with each other. That's another skill that is important in relationships.

If you're the person who has less availability, notice whether your prospective date pouts or puts you down. That's a behavior that won't change, I promise you. If you're the person who has fewer commitments, decide whether you're comfortable fitting into someone else's calendar. If he doesn't have time to get together *whenever*, that's not going to change either. You're not college kids, who can meet up anytime they don't have homework. When you date as an adult, you're dating each other's schedules, too.

With that in mind, assess whether planning dates is going to be a hassle in the future, and decide whether you want to save yourself the headache! Nothing is worse than getting attached to someone who is into you but isn't capable of giving you the time and attention you deserve.

Do's and Don'ts for a Perfect First Date

Dr. Gluck: What are the ingredients of romance? Candlelight, wine, good food, and flowing conversation. These elements should be in balance to create a perfect evening. As we said, when the balance is right, time stops existing. You don't look at your phone. You don't even look at your watch! By the time the check comes, you should feel emotionally satisfied. You clicked. The chemistry was right: this is a person you'd like to get to know.

Rori: Oh, Dr. G. You make it sound so simple. A good date will definitely go smoothly. It will feel natural, just like flirting. When it's right, it's right. But when it's wrong, be grateful you saved yourself wasted time and aggravation.

One awkward moment is not the end of the world, though. I was on a date once, and I thought I looked really good. I was so excited about my outfit: I found these Gucci leather pants marked way, way, way on sale. They were like 90 percent off! It didn't matter that they were a size thirty-eight and I am a real size forty. I squeezed my ass into them and went out. Everything was fine until I went to the bathroom and I couldn't get it up—my zipper, that is! I flipped. I went back to the table and said, "I need your blazer *immediately*. Take it off *now*."

My date was like, what? But he gave me the jacket and we got out of there, fast! It became something we could laugh about, because I treated the moment with humor instead of letting it ruin our night.

Dr. Gluck: There are plenty of ways to derail the magic. When one of our clients checks in after a date and says they just didn't feel the attraction, we ask why. The answers are almost always the same. The conversation was boring, the other person didn't seem interested, or the other person was not at *all* who they seemed to be.

The first two problems are easy to fix: they are issues of focus. As we mentioned in the first chapter, body language is important to maintaining your personal chemistry. If you invite someone to a lovely dinner and then spend the whole time rolling your eyes or staring at the TV in the corner, you're telling them you find them boring and unattractive. Pay attention to your date. If distraction is an issue for you, choose a restaurant that doesn't have a TV on the wall. Ask to be seated against the wall and select a chair that faces away from the center of the room. That way, you can give your date your undivided attention. This may not always be possible, but you must make it a priority, or you risk missing out on a wonderful time because you couldn't control your wandering eyes.

Rori: Conversation is like flirting—it's a game, it's fun, and it shouldn't feel like a chore. If you sit down at the table and suddenly everything you say is simply not being heard, switch tactics. Ask your date questions—without cross-examining them! Maybe you can find out where they went to school, where they're from. Fill in the blanks of what you already know.

This is another thing that dating sites won't give you: the mystery of getting to know someone. On a person's online profile, they'll put *so* much information about themselves. But that doesn't tell you anything about who they really are, what they care about, or how they ended up where they are today. The first date allows you to explore each other's personalities. It's a fact-finding mission. Of course, just play it cool. Ask questions like a sexy detective—not an FBI agent!

Dr. Gluck: Be aware of how your date responds, and how they're feeling. Mutual respect and attention should get you through any awkward moments.

Rori: Unless there's a disaster.

Dr. Gluck: Disasters can be managed, though. I suggest that the only true dating disaster is the situation that you failed to handle with humor, maturity, and grace.

Rori: Yes, there's nothing worse than a date with someone who acts like a spoiled child. The biggest turn-off? Being rude to the waiter. Oh, my God! That drives me crazy. If your date treats service people like that, what makes you think they'll treat you any better? A guy who leaves a bad tip, or sends his meal back four times, or has unrealistic expectations about the service, is telling you *all* you need to know.

The first date is the audition. You're screening each other, in some ways. Is Mister Handsome so good-looking when you get him under the microscope? Or does he spend an hour talking trash about his first wife, complaining about child support? Does he hold forth about topics that only *he* knows about, like the fantasy football draft picks and his job? That's boring. Guys who do that are really saying, "I'm not looking for a partner, I'm looking for an audience." I say, next!

Dr. Gluck: In reality TV, dating is often portrayed as a tournament. From *The Dating Game* to *The Real Housewives of New York* and *The Bachelor*, dates are expected to compete for each other's attention and use all the tools of charm that are at their disposal. The smallest infraction, whether it's a bad tie or bad breath, can get someone eliminated. You screw up, and you're out.

Rori: Real life dating is hopefully not as cutthroat. It's supposed to be fun. Of course, you don't compromise your desires or your boundaries: if you're supposed to have dinner at Per Se, and your date shows up in Birkenstocks and a baseball cap, that's enough of a reason to pass on them. But a conversational misstep or a minor mistake, like accidentally stumbling onto a sensitive subject, shouldn't be taken too seriously. It's still early: you're getting to know each other. Don't sweat the small stuff. Focus on getting to know what your date is really about.

What's little to one person is big to another, though. If you're coming from a divorce, for example, it might drive you *crazy* to see your date doing something that your ex-wife or ex-husband did. Be honest with yourself about your deal breakers. Do you really want to end up with another woman who checks her makeup at the table or a guy who scarfs down all the dessert, without sharing? Remember, this is your *life*. You're allowed to be picky!

It may feel a little awkward to turn down a second date with someone who reminds you a little too much of the ex you love to hate, but you're doing yourself—and them—a favor in the long run. It's one thing to have a type. It's another to set yourself up for a decade of feeling resentful.

Each date isn't an elimination round, but I'll tell you, from a common sense perspective, if you encounter a quality in the other person that just isn't working for you, let them go. Whatever you learn about them, you can assume it's not going to change. They're not going to suddenly start caring about politics or the stock market or any *other* thing in which you're deeply interested. They're not going to transform into your perfect mate, if you just give them the time. That kind of thinking wastes weeks, months, and even years that you could spend looking for, and dating, your soulmate!

Personalities and preferences don't change. Instead of compromising your way into yet another dead-end relationship, stick to your ideals Your gut knows what's up: trust that bitch.

Don't Touch That Check

Dr. Gluck: Another effect of increasing equality for women is this trend of going Dutch. Women are more empowered sexually, which means that they are more likely to make the first move, speak up about their desires in a relationship, and be the one to ask you on a date. They're also more empowered financially. Platinum Poire matches elite clients, from New York's one percent. They can afford to pay for their own dinner! With that said, when the check comes, should they be the one to pay?

Rori: Absolutely *not*. Ladies, don't you touch that check. I don't care how liberated you are. That is the man's obligation, and it should be his pleasure.

Let me tell you something about men, if you haven't already figured it out. Men like to feel like *men*. When a man is comfortable with himself, his masculinity, he is happier. He works better, plays better, and is more fun to be around. A man who likes to be manly is sexy, too. Admit it: those old-fashioned manners are a turn-on! One of the oldest man-moves in the book is picking up the check. When you let him do this, you're affirming his masculinity. You're allowing him to be *the man*. Don't take that away from him, just because you want to prove a point about being a feminist or whatever.

Dr. Gluck: Modern etiquette dictates that whoever asks, pays. That means that if you invite your date to a charming, exclusive restaurant in Midtown, you should be prepared to pick up the check. It would be rude to ask and then expect the other person to foot the bill. With that said, the first date can be an exception. On the first date, there should be no arguing about whose credit card gets charged. There should also be no power struggle over splitting the check, or nickel-and-diming your beautiful, romantic evening into a financial transaction. That kills the mood.

On the first date, the man should always offer to pay. If you continue seeing each other, and get to know each other better, it can be appropriate to split up the tab then. Lunches, coffee dates, and other small charges can be split. But let this first night out be romantic. It's a time to enjoy each other, not fight about money.

Rori: A gentleman knows he's paying for dinner. It's part of the deal. I've heard some women say, "If he pays for my dinner, he's going to want something in return." To that, I say, "If you knew that when he asked you, why did you agree to the date?" Dating is not about getting anything from the other person, other than a pleasant evening together.

The other complaint I hear from men is, "Why should I spend money on a woman I might never see again? It's a scam!" Guys who think like that have a terrible time finding a girlfriend because they don't understand that they're not paying for a woman's attention. Look, your date is not a stripper. She is not on the clock. She's not in it for the food. She is your *date*, and when you pick up the tab, you're demonstrating to her that you know how to show her a good time. You don't take someone to an amusement park and then make them pay for every ride! Paying for the first date dinner is not a *trade*. It is a *gift*. Smart women understand this, and smart men pay without complaining or being crude.

When All Else Fails, Send Flowers

Dr. Gluck: No matter how well you plan, things can go badly. Very badly. Remember every date is an appointment of which both parties are seeing whether they can strike a deal.

Rori: Is anything worse than a first-date disaster? The food is bad, you run into your ex, you spill your drink in your lap (or better yet on his lap), your jokes fall flat, you have a wardrobe malfunction. There is a long list of things that can throw off your night. Some of those things are distressing, and some can be laughed off. The real question is, did it throw your date off?

Dr. Gluck: The rational and reliable go-to is *don't text*. Pick up the phone and talk. All real love comes out of real communication.

Rori: If you completely screwed up and you still want to see the person again, you need to make an effort. Send a bouquet, with a note saying that you weren't at your best. Let them know you'd like another chance. Flowers don't fix everything—but they sure won't make things worse.

Here's the checklist for a platinum first date:

➤ Commit to a date and time that works for both of you.

➤ Make a reservation for two at a restaurant with which you're familiar and that you can afford.

➤ Show up on time, looking your best, with a good attitude.

➤ Listen to your date, ask questions, and get to know them. Try to listen as much as you speak, so you don't monopolize the conversation.

➤ When the check comes, the man pays. This is not up for debate!

➤ Walk your date to their car or wait with them for their cab.

➤ The next morning, send flowers if you screwed up. If you had a wonderful time, a phone call thanking them for a nice evening is a great way to show your appreciation—and maybe even make plans for next time.

Dr. Gluck: After a couple of months of dating, kissing, and spending time together, you should have a solid idea of who this new, exciting person is. Dating sustains your chemistry, allowing you to learn more and explore this new relationship as it develops.

Now, this is obviously dependent on you and your partner. If you're seeing each other every Saturday, you might need less time to make your next decision than if you go on two dates a month or less. Ballpark, you should know within three dates whether you'd like to keep seeing each other. You'll know within a month or two whether you'd like to date them seriously. That becomes a truer statement for those who have been around the block (not every block). When you meet someone who captivates you, the first bonds of intimacy start to form. That's emotional monogamy: the feeling that you want to be exclusive with this person.

Rori: Up to the point of commitment, it's okay to date more than one person at a time. You can play the field, even, as long as you're honest with the people you're seeing. When one of those relationships starts to deepen, pull back and reassess what you're doing. Are you sleeping with one person, when you really want to be dating a different one? Are you seeing someone about whom you don't feel warmly, just because they're available and giving you attention?

Remember, you want to *commit without compromise*. You don't want just any relationship; you want the *right* relationship. The first three months of dates is your trial run. You're testing to see if the person is worthy of meeting your family, friends, children, and colleagues. Can they go the distance? At any time, you can change your mind and walk away—which is not hard to do, as long as you don't become too attached. Once your heart is involved, it can be difficult to make decisions with your brain. You can decide whether you want to pursue this connection.

The point is to keep your eyes open and make smart choices *before* you catch any feelings. It's hard to keep the bar high when you've got a crush on your date. I will tell you that lowering that bar is never a good idea. You'll end up in a relationship, but at the cost of your dreams. Think long term and put yourself first.

If you move forward, you're not just going on dates. You're *dating*.

Congratulations! You're one step closer to the platinum pair of your dreams.

Chapter 6

Jealousy is a Spice, Not a Stand-Alone Dish

So, you've been dating for a few months—*exclusively*. You introduce your partner as your girlfriend or boyfriend. You might be thinking that you'd like to include them in a family gathering, or a work function. When they walk into a room, you feel that *zazazou*. Wow! Their smile, their laugh, and your special inside jokes are all so meaningful to you. So what happens when you see them laughing or smiling with someone else?

We all have experience with jealousy, the green-eyed monster that lives inside of every one of us. The jealousy in your relationship can add zing or poison the entire meal. Jealousy, as a relationship dynamic, is incredibly unhealthy. It can tear a couple apart. However, feeling a little bit jealous is also a sign that you're invested in your partner. It's a sign that you want to feel committed, and in some cases, that it's time to move forward aggressively in the relationship.

In this chapter, Dr. Gluck and Rori explain what good, bad, and ugly jealousy look like. This chapter includes some activities to help you work through your jealousy and address the beliefs or blocks underneath envious or jealous emotions.

Wandering Eyes and Hands

Dr. Gluck: Humans are social. In New York, especially, we're around other people all the time. Because our brains respond to visual stimuli, it's natural to notice and be noticed by others as well. Flirting plays with that connection. Yet, you don't want to flirt with everyone. You don't necessarily want attention from everyone, either. As your emotional attachment to your partner grows, you may sense new boundaries in your relationship. If you were formerly very flirty and open to talking to many different kinds of people, your sexual energy may now feel more focused on your partner. One aspect of emotional monogamy—flirting or engaging in social contact that has a sexual charge—that becomes suddenly less appealing.

This transition to emotional monogamy isn't a sign that you're shutting down, sexually. Your chemistry is still there. It's still vital, powerful, and part of your identity. What's happening is that your emotions become involved. You may be developing serious feelings about your partner. Your brain is choosing to focus on that person, giving them all the attention you might have previously divided between multiple dates or flirting partners. The transition is usually marked by a feeling that you are no longer interested in playing the field.

Rori: Once you've crossed the line into emotional monogamy, it's very hard to turn back. This is why we tell you to go slow! An emotional attachment is serious because that's where love begins. If you want to develop a healthy, lasting love, you start with good ingredients. You can't make challah with stale flour, rancid butter, and dusty raisins, right? Love is the same. You make it fresh. You also don't share that love with everyone on the block. Your love is precious, and your heart knows that. Although flirting and going on dates is light and fun, at some point you won't feel right sharing yourself with two, three, or ten people. You'll notice yourself gravitating toward one of them. They make you laugh the most. They hold you close and leave you tingling all over. They're the one you call or text when you have good news to share. Those are signs that you've found someone special, who you're eager to be with.

You treat that person differently than the others. They're your special guy, your person, and hopefully, they feel the same way about you! So, how do you feel when you see your honey chatting up the cute hostess at your favorite lunch spot? *Jealous.* Your sweetie's actions violate the emotional connection you're forming, and you might even feel threatened. You might feel insecure, too: what does that other person have that's so captivating? Either way, the green-eyed monster is awake—and she can be *real* bitch.

Dr. Gluck: In nature, animals fight tooth and claw over potential mates. For example, two brightly colored birds will tear each other's feathers out, trying to drive away a sexual competitor. Some animals, like primates, will even kill one another out of jealousy. It is one of our most primal emotions and is an instinctive response to a threat. No matter how culturally or socially evolved humans may be, we all have the capacity to experience jealousy.

Rori: Anyone who tells you they "don't get jealous" is lying. For men, physical contact with a man is usually the trigger. They might see their girlfriend hugging or kissing another guy or giving him special attention that seems a little too friendly. She might linger too long, or let this other man hold her coat for her, or her bag. It crosses a physical line that makes you uncomfortable. Without that kiss or hug, however, the interaction is kosher.

For women, it's the emotional gestures that cause problems. The suggestion that the boyfriend is emotionally intimate with other women creates intense jealousy. For example, let's say that your boyfriend spends time on the phone with his close, female friend. When she calls, he leaves the other room to talk to her—and closes the door. This creates jealousy. You wonder: *What are they talking about? Why is he laughing? Why aren't I included?*

Dr. Gluck: Jealousy can be unhealthy, or it can intensify your connection. Obviously, negative jealousy is not something you want. If someone uses their jealousy to control your choices or act in ways that are frightening or abusive, that's a sign to leave the relationship immediately. If you experience jealousy that is challenging or an obvious sign of codependency, that's enough reason to leave the relationship immediately.

Jealousy that adds spice is different. It originates from an emotional attachment to your partner, not a desire to limit or control them. It also means you might need to redefine your boundaries with people who are not your partner, to avoid blow-ups that undermine your relationship.

If one person is feeling jealous, and the other defends their actions without apologizing, saying "it's no big deal," that's a sign of an imbalance in the relationship. It shows that the attachment between you is lopsided.

Rori: I disagree. I think a good relationship makes you free, and you can flirt without making your partner feel threatened. Flirty behavior is totally appropriate *outside* the relationship. Why shouldn't you have fun? You're just playing, meeting people, and having a good time. But once you're committed, and forming those intimate bonds, the rules change.

Flirting often when you're single lets others know you are single. You might even do it once you're dating someone. But let me tell you, once those boundaries are established, you better not cross them!

Dr. Gluck: Communicating about the jealousy can help you connect in a healthy way. Whether you are the partner experiencing jealousy, or the one causing it, listen to what you're both feeling. Here are some questions you can ask yourself if you're experiencing jealous feelings:

> Is my jealousy based in reality?
> What is the fear behind my jealousy? Why do I feel this way?
> Can I communicate about my emotions clearly, without downplaying how I feel?
> If my partner continues this behavior after I've asked them to change or made my feelings clear, how will I respond?
> If they're not willing to change, am I willing to keep having this argument for the duration of the relationship?

If you're the person who is causing the jealous feelings, you also have a part to play. Here are some questions that you can use to work through this situation:

> ➤ Did I cause these jealous feelings by accident, or on purpose? If it was intentional, what did I hope to gain?

> ➤ How does my partner's jealousy make me feel? Why?

> ➤ Am I willing to change my behavior? Why or why not?

> ➤ If I'm not willing to change, am I willing to keep having this argument for the duration of the relationship?

A Dance with the Green-Eyed Monster

Dr. Gluck: Men and women get jealous for different reasons, about different issues. One has to look at jealousy as a function of your lack of personal self-esteem. If your partner is hugging and kissing a friends that you don't know and that makes you jealous, you either have a trust issue or you're simply with the wrong person. The relationship dynamic won't change, no matter how jealous one might get.

Let me be clear. Jealousy is a disease, not a desire. It should never escalate to physical or verbal abuse. Just like flirting, it is simply a means of communication. Everyone has different communication styles. A man is not necessarily a pig for flirting, just like a woman who does it isn't a whore. I'll give you a hint: real players are so smooth they don't arouse jealousy at all. That's how they're able to keep doing what they do and get away with it.

Rori: If it bothers you, say something. Each couple must define their limits. Some people can handle having a partner who's touchy-feely with others, or who has friends of the opposite sex. Some people don't mind their boyfriends hanging around with women they used to screw, or even sending flowers to former girlfriends. I can tell you right now, that's a non-starter for me. It's a great way to get me to lose your phone number!

The point is that what works for one couple, works for them. What works for one *person* in the couple had better work for *both* of the people in it. You can't have one partner creating drama, causing jealousy, and then telling the other person to just get over it. Relationships don't work that way. They're built on clear communication and mutual respect.

Dr. Gluck: But there are some situations where a little jealousy is exciting. Consensual jealousy can set the stage for intensified feelings. For example, if you have a "no heavy flirting" boundary in your relationship, your partner might choose to play with that in order to arouse you. Imagine that you're watching your partner at a party. She looks over her shoulder at you, tosses her hair flirtatiously, and then puts her hand on the arm of the man she's talking to. Another man! That would certainly get my attention but not necessarily in a negative way.

In this situation, your girlfriend is telling you, loud and clear, that she knows how to get you worked up. She didn't cross a line with this other guy, out of respect for you. She also *could have gone further if she wanted.* This kind of jealousy that you feel is exciting because you're a part of the interaction. She was flirting in order to be seen, knowing that her behavior would get a rise out of you.

Rori: Using your partner's jealousy is a little risky. Some people hate it, and others can't get enough. These kinds of games are based on mutual trust: you know your partner would never cross the line, even though they might play with those limits. The big word here is *consent*. When you make someone jealous on purpose, it should be because you know it will get them going, in a good way.

Jealousy can be something that comes up indirectly. In one couple I know, the woman has a male friend at her job that she refers to as her "work husband." Her actual husband has met this coworker, likes him, and doesn't feel threatened. He teases her about this "work husband," and the friendship is a little bit of a joke between them. There's no question that it's not anything more than a working relationship. The closeness that his wife shares with this other guy isn't a problem, but it does remind him that his wife is attractive, and that she has meaningful friendships with men that are deep and still in the Friend Zone.

Dr. Gluck: Yes, seeing other people respond to your partner can help remind you of the chemistry that drew you to them in the first place. Over time, it's easy to get complacent in a relationship. You see each other frequently; you go to the same bars, shows, and restaurants; you find a rhythm together. Those patterns are special because they're particular to you. They can also dull the attraction, because they're familiar. You know what your partner looks like in the morning, before they brush their teeth. In the first three months, you'll probably see their home, and learn a few things about how they live in private. That's intimacy. A partner who knows how to work the room keeps your attraction hot. Seeing or hearing your partner work their charm on someone else reminds you:

this is the sexy, interesting person to whom I couldn't wait to talk.

Rori: Just save some of that magic for your partner. If you're giving it to the bartender, you should definitely give it to your boyfriend. That's what jealousy does: it reminds your partner what you have, and then it gives them a little reward. Never forget, no matter how much fun she seems to be having with that new VP of Sales, she's going home with *you*. And that can be very sexy. Remember: he's only the appetizer, you partner is the main dish.

Green Is *So* Not Your Color

Dr. Gluck: Destructive jealousy is less subtle. It hurts. It's a negative feeling. It starts in the gut and makes you feel queasy. Your mind might start to race, creating imaginary scenarios about what your partner is doing, who they're with, and why they haven't checked in. Unchecked jealousy can escalate to rage and lead to the kinds of fights from which are hard to recover. Yet, so many of these arguments could have been avoided with better communication.

Rori: My rule is, *do unto others as you would like done unto you*. In a relationship, I model the kind of behavior I would like my partner to show me. If I'm not dishing about my ex and the sex-life I had with him, I definitely don't want to hear my current boyfriend sharing all the dirty details with me. If I commit to someone and decide to dial down the flirting to just a few key, safe male friends, I'd expect my partner to do the same. By the same token, if my boyfriend changes his social habits as he becomes more intimate with me, I notice and I follow his lead. It's a

109

dance. I don't do the things that will make my partner upset and unhappy, and if he's a gentleman, he'll make an effort to do the same.

Dr. Gluck: Deliberately ignoring your partner's cues is a guaranteed way to hurt their feelings, and maybe even lose their trust. Ideally, they will be able to say, "I don't like it when you do that," but not all people communicate these things verbally. If you're suddenly faced with your partner's jealousy, and it came out of left field, it's time to have an adult conversation. You don't want to hurt them, and they probably don't want to feel like they have to manipulate you in order to get their needs met. Take the lead. Putting it out on the table and being willing to make some concessions—that is, changing your behavior—can end up helping your relationship and your intimacy grow.

Rori: If he does something hurtful on purpose continually, after that conversation—down the rabbit hole he goes!

Dr. Gluck: Yes, taking advantage of your partner's jealousy to create negative feelings is a sign that you're not ready for a relationship. Obsession, insecurity, and lack of trust kill romance. That's not a healthy foundation on which to build a life together. If you find yourself stirring the pot, acting out with your sexuality, or trying to rile your partner up, it's time to get some professional help. Learn why you are attracted to codependent behaviors and how to have healthier connections with the people you love.

Rori: We said it before: real life is not reality TV. Someone who is so fun to watch, a total drama magnet, is not someone you want to date—much less marry! If you find yourself going back for seconds after your partner

110

treats you badly, check yourself. Is this how you want your love story to be? If not, there's plenty of potential mates out there who are going to treat you 100 percent better. Get what you deserve. You never have to settle.

Social Media is Definitely the Devil

Rori: Dating apps are the devil. They nip romance in the bud, they're totally fake, and they don't even work the majority of the time. But if Tinder and OKCupid are bad for relationships, social media apps are even worse. Nothing creates jealousy faster than a peek at someone's Facebook page. Suddenly, you can see *way* more of their personal life. You catch yourself clicking through their photos. They went *where*? *When*? With *who*?

Social media feeds our negative obsession and jealous feelings. That's why you need to be extra careful with how you portray yourself online. Your partner should be aware of themselves, too. It might seem petty, but the smallest comment or click can turn into a *big* problem.

Dr. Gluck: I hate to say it, but perception is everything. Social media can complicate our perceptions of one another. The things you share can give a false impression of what you're really up to. Guys are more prone to this, because they just don't think it through. Checking into a restaurant, posting a photo of yourself with another woman (even if she's just a friend), or sharing a fun moment from your night can spark jealousy in your partner.

Now, I'm not suggesting that you hide what you're doing. It's not a good to fall into that kind of habit. But be mindful of your partner's feelings, whether you're online or not. If you plan to meet up with an old girlfriend for lunch, and your current partner knows, that's fine—but you may not want to post a cute selfie with your former flame. A little foresight can prevent unhappiness down the line.

Rori: You might be thinking, *it's Facebook, who cares?* Umm, how about *everyone?* Social media is part of how we communicate now. It's not just millennials and younger people: it's for people in their fifties, sixties, and older, too. Although everyone uses social media a little differently, the fact is that it's part of how you share yourself with the world. And your partner may not be thrilled if you're sharing certain things—not just with them, but with your family, friends, coworkers, and the entire internet. Your online behavior is just as important as what you do in life.

You can have an honest conversation with your partner about how you'd like to conduct your relationship online. Let's be real, it doesn't feel good to see this stuff pop up on your screen. It *really* doesn't feel good to be the person who's digging through your partner's profile, either. That's not the fun kind of jealousy. It's the kind that hurts.

Here's an example. If you've committed to your partner, and part of that commitment is no longer meeting up with your ex for coffee or texting them all the time, you should probably not have a lively online friendship with that person. Some people would say it's not that big a deal. I think it is. If your boyfriend tells you he's no longer speaking to his former fuck-buddy, but you can see that he's "liking" all her sexy photos on Instagram, that's a problem. It shows that your boyfriend's actions are not consistent with the words he's telling you. Now, this doesn't 100 percent mean he's cheating—but it means he needs to change his behavior if he wants to earn your trust.

Basically, the promises you make to each other don't end when you log on to social media. Think about how your clicks and comments make you look: committed, or a creep?

Keep That Monster Locked in the Closet

Dr. Gluck: What causes jealousy? It's an innate part of being human. Anyone who wants to make their jealousy magically go away is really asking, "How can I be less human?" It's not realistic to expect to go through life without some jealousy.

I always say, "It's not how you feel, it's what you do about it." How you handle your feelings, whether they're negative or positive, can lead you to more personal growth—and better relationships in the long run.

Rori: Jealousy isn't something you can get rid of just by wishing you didn't feel that way. Don't try pretending you aren't bothered by something that really gets you mad. You can't sweep jealousy under the rug or stuff it in the closet. That is only going to make it worse.

What you can do is laugh about it and take it in stride. For example, I was on a date with my husband. We're at a nice place, having fun, and suddenly the waiter came over with a note and a bottle of wine. He said, "A woman at another table wanted to give you this."

The note was her phone number! I was like, "Bitch, he is *on a date* and you send him a note? I'm sitting right here!" My head snapped around like *The Exorcist*. But Charles and I laughed it off, and the Desperate Debbie who tried to pick him up has become a joke between us. I could have let that ruin my evening, but it was just so ridiculous, I had to laugh.

Dr. Gluck: To cope with jealousy, whether it's the thrilling kind or the kind that makes you sick to your stomach, you need to check in with yourself. What's creating this feeling? Addressing the root causes of your jealousy will help you see what steps to take next, with your partner and yourself. Jealousy sends a message that may not always be clear, even though it's certainly loud. Here are some questions that will help you discern what it is trying to tell you:

> When was the last time I felt this way?
> What specifically triggered this feeling of jealousy?
> Do I believe my partner has a motive or intention behind their action? If so, what is it?
> Am I reacting to my partner's perceived motive, their action, or both?
> Is this jealousy a turn-off or a turn-on? Why?
> Do I feel like my partner's actions are depriving me of something I should have for myself? What am I missing out on?
> In my ideal relationship, jealousy is

_____.

Rori: In healthy relationships, there's going to be some jealousy. It's natural and normal. When you feel jealous, that emotion doesn't come out of nowhere! You don't have to be powerless just because you have this feeling. You can use it to fine-tune and enhance your relationship and make it even better than before. It can even add some spice to your love life!

Learning about those limits and boundaries is so important to build a lasting relationship. So don't fear jealousy. You can collar that green-eyed monster, and make it work for *you*.

Chapter 7

Mastering the Art of the Relationship

Dating is an art form that extends into the life long relationship. A relationship grows from your *firsts*: the first smile, first conversation, first date, first kiss. From the first date, to the special time you spend getting to know each other, you're practicing the skills that will sustain romance over time.

The honeymoon period sets the stage for the rest of your lives together. This is a time of growth, both individually and together. Who are you, as a couple? Can you find a healthy balance? What does your shared future hold? If you've started your new relationship with a clear sense of who you are and what you need, you are off to a good start. The art of the relationship requires awareness and intention.

Relating to other people takes practice, especially when you're adding someone new to your life. However, a healthy relationship shouldn't feel like an uphill battle. When you master the art of the relationship, you're not only going to improve the relationship you're building. You will gain a better understanding of yourself and what you need in order to be happy. You'll also become better at discerning when it's not working, and when to back off, or even walk away.

Every relationship goes through the same stages. At any point, if it's not right, you can make a change. Someone who understands relationships is confident enough to ask for what they want. They never settle for less. In this chapter, Rori and Dr. Gluck explain how to apply your dating skills to maintaining your new relationship with your partner. Your boundaries, changing friendships, staying out of the Friend Zone, and new priorities are all key to staying happy as you grow romantically.

Boundaries Make the Heart Grow Fonder

Dr. Gluck: In the first blush of new love, it can be very tempting to overshare. When you meet someone and like them, you naturally want to connect. You want to spend tons of time together, tell them all about yourself, and share the special things in your life. Realistic expectations and healthy boundaries will keep your new relationship growing.

Rori: We've all been there. The first date, sparks are flying, the wine is flowing, and you are feeling so familiar and you are just doing you. The next thing you know, you're spilling about your divorce, your last girlfriend, your family drama, and your deepest, darkest secrets. All the things you say to your therapist, you're now saying to your date. And you wonder why your phone doesn't ring!

Even if the other person is feeling that attraction, an information dump is going to ruin it. So much of dating is the mystery, the gradual discovery of the other person. Dating is about maintaining that chemistry and that tension. Too much information is a *no*. No matter how tempting it is, keep your mouth shut! You just met this person. They don't need to hear all about your adolescence or your ex-husband's weird control issues. They need to get to know *you.*

Dr. Gluck: Set some ground rules for yourself, especially for the first few dates. Your boundaries are going to be specific to you: for example, you may not want to share that your second child was conceived through IVF, but you're happy to tell your date that you are a proud parent of three college-aged kids. You may want to avoid mentioning your net worth until after a few months, when you have the talk about financial compatibility. But it's perfectly fine to talk about your job and what you do for a living, in a general way.

Try to establish boundaries that allow you to share information about yourself without putting pressure on the other person. One of our clients, for example, was raising a special needs child at home. She was open about this and shared that part of her life with all of her dates. She knew that was important, because she was looking for a husband—someone who would be fully part of her life. She wanted a partner who would honor her commitment to her child and value what a dedicated, involved mother she was.

Now, for many men, this was a deal-breaker. She never made it to the second date with them. They heard "special needs" and ran. And that's a good thing, because she shouldn't ever have to apologize for her child or hide something that is such a big part of her life. She deserves to have a partner who sees her child as a blessing, not a liability. It hurt her feelings to feel rejected, but she didn't compromise. The *right* guy stuck around. She's now happily married to him: a man who adores her and her child, and they're a family. Boundaries helped her find a committed, loving, supportive relationship.

Rori: Your date is not your closest girlfriend. If you want to gush about your new promotion or process a past relationship—do it with them. It's not appropriate to do that to your date. They hardly know you! What will they think if all you do is gossip about yourself and the people you know? That's not very romantic. Even if they find you sexy, that attraction won't last long if they have to hear all about your feud with your best friend. Eventually, your date will hear about that stuff, if they stick around. They might even meet the best friend in question. But that's *later*.

Online dating profiles encourage oversharing. People put all kinds of information out there, for anyone to see. Every little thing, from vacation photos to where you went to college. It takes the fun out of meeting someone and it ruins the chemistry. You're dating a person, not their resume.

Make the person earn your trust. Give them a chance to open up. Let them develop an interest. Sustain that curiosity. Just as you wouldn't sleep with someone on the first date, you wouldn't show them your emotional panties, either. That's a great way to scare someone off. Instead of going home at the end of the night feeling butterflies, they'll be thinking, "She's certifiable." That's not the goal. You can open up without overdoing it.

Dr. Gluck: Disclosure of any personal information is always your own choice. Bear in mind that, if you've been set up by friends, you and your date may already know a little about each other. You might know them casually from flirting. That doesn't matter. Come to the table fresh.

Whether you like them or not, this is a stranger. They're new in your life.

Rori: On the other hand, you don't need to lie. Dating someone means you'll eventually get through the whole list of important stuff: sex, money, values, family, spirituality, home, work, vacations. I think it's wrong to hold back something that would significantly impact the relationship down the line, if it wasn't known. For example, if you're in the middle of a complicated lawsuit, you should probably bring that up. If you just lost a parent to a long illness, that's good to mention too.

If you've put in the work to get healthy, emotionally and financially, *before* you go on the hunt for a partner, you'll be able to avoid awkward conversations.

Dr. Gluck: Yes, if you're currently mid-divorce, I question why you'd be dating seriously. It's the same as dating when your financial life is a mess. Why would you want to bring another person into that situation? Now, we all have unresolved issues—unanswered questions—that crop up throughout our lives. Have clear boundaries for yourself and make sure you're in good shape to add another person to your life.

Rori: Especially for people who haven't dated in decades, dating without drama might be a new concept. It's not impossible! Most of the problems come when you bring up sex too soon or overshare about your love life. Look, sex is part of a relationship. You will probably end up sleeping with the person you date at some point, once you've gotten to know each other. Ask yourself: are they going to want to sleep with you if they've already heard all about where you've been, and what you've done? No. That is a turn-off. It's not exciting to listen to your date's exploits.

If I'm going out with a guy, the focus is on *him*. I don't want to hear about how his last girlfriend had no gag reflex, or how he's so studly he needs two or three women at a time. Deal breaker! I would not go back for seconds, and I definitely would not sleep with him. Why? Because I know that if he's saying this stuff about his other girlfriends, he'll definitely say it about me, too. What you choose to share with your date says plenty about your character. A romantic dinner is not a locker room and it's *not* a session with your best friends. The goal is to make your date feel special and learn more about them. I don't want to hear about the blowjob queen that broke your heart three years ago.

If you think you can sit next to me for an hour and tell me all about your ex, I'm going to tell you straight up, "She was right to leave you, you big baby! After an hour of your bullshit, I'm leaving too!" Get real! You need to be in therapy, not looking for love.

It's a Jungle Out There

Dr. Gluck: At Platinum Poire, we recommend an old-fashioned approach to dating, using tried-and-true methods that build intimacy over time. The first date is a big hurdle for many people. There's so much preparation and anticipation. When it goes well, you know you're on your way to finding a meaningful connection to someone special. The next step is, well, the second date. And the third date. And the fourth, and so on.

Now, the first date is a courtship ritual that has a fairly rigid structure. What you talk about and how is important. Over time, as you warm up to one another, you'll want to start leaving that structure behind and exploring other kinds of dates as well.

Rori: Not that it's a bad thing to keep having dinner together! Having "your" special place to connect, revisit those first-date flutters, and share a dessert is very sweet. It creates a mini tradition in the relationship, which is part of intimacy.

Dr. Gluck: Yes, that first night out is an important element in the relationship. Hopefully, it's the first of many. When you make positive memories with another person, you're growing together. That's why we emphasize formality, especially when you're beginning to date. The structure of the first date makes it a very safe, low-stakes environment to test the waters. If it doesn't work out, then you've had a good meal in the company of someone with whom you didn't click. No loss. After that foundation of trust is formed, however, it's time to explore other options.

Rori: When you marry someone, you're committing to someone you love, accept, and trust. I mean *deep* trust. Don't commit until you've gotten to know each other in different ways. That's what dating is for! It's a long audition that shows you what the other person is really like, what is meaningful and important to them, and how they behave in different scenarios. You want to see their true colors *before* you even think about putting a ring on it.

Now, since life is not a dating show, you don't want to throw your date into the deep end. Bungee jumping, scuba diving, extreme sports—forget about it! If that's not your partner's thing, don't push it. You can get to know someone without diving off a cliff or making them pet a shark. Dating is exciting enough—you don't need to add a near death experience.

One of my exes was a real adrenaline junkie. His idea of a fun date was going off-roading, zip-lining, or skydiving. I'm *not* going off-roading. Do you even know me? My idea of a fun date is the theater, a museum, or Rosè all day. This Prada-wearing, polished princess was not having it. I was like, "My neck is going to snap."

It's fine if climbing Mount Everest is your thing. It's just not mine. Did this guy know who he was dating? Clearly not. We were clearly not a fit.

Dr. Gluck: Adrenaline can overpower endorphins and oxytocin, the feel-good hormones that create a sense of love in your brain. In dating, focus on your partner's character, not their survival skills. If a guy is an alpha male, you'll be able to tell by the way he dresses, behaves, and treats you. No need to make him arm-wrestle a gorilla! Find the right balance of romance and fun that let you learn what your partner is like in different situations. The odds that you'll be stranded in the Arctic with your partner are slim to nonexistent, so why worry about skills or activities that have no bearing on the life you'll share together?

We have a few suggestions for people who are comfortable with the traditional aspects of dating and are ready to take the next steps. Now, this is *after* you have that foundation of trust that is so important. You don't want to throw the person into the deep end. That's not fair to them, and it's a recipe for disaster. Once you know a little more about who they are, and whether you want to date seriously, you can start learning what they're really about.

Rori: If you do it right, you can learn so much about someone, just on the first date. Any time you're around them, talking, flirting, spending time together, whatever, you're picking up new information. When you both go out of your comfort zone—even a tiny bit—it gives you both the opportunity to really open up. Here are a few date ideas that will give you the chance to get to know your date better:

The Best Things in Life are Free
Go on a date where you both agree not to spend money. What can you do for free? A long walk, a free public lecture or reading, or even cooking a dinner together are interesting ways to spend a few hours together. It also puts the emphasis on the person's creativity: can they have fun without spending any money, or do they need to pay to play? Is it fun to talk to them, without distractions? Also this kind of date can help you learn if you are attracted to one another *without* finances being involved. If you can only enjoy your date's company when they're treating you to a nice dinner, a helicopter ride, a night on the town, or the theater—you're probably not attracted to them as a person.

Remember that money comes and goes. Most people experience financial changes over the duration of their lives. The economy changes, and unless a person is in the one percent, they'll probably feel the pinch at some point. Wealth is a nice benefit in a relationship, but it cannot be the bedrock of your commitment to each other.

I mean, it's easy to get all misty-eyed about old people holding hands and walking through the park together. You think this happened overnight? No. Being married for forty, fifty, or sixty years means a decades of conversations and mornings doing the crossword together. Give it a try. If it drives you crazy now, you probably won't like in fifty years, either.

Give Back and Give Love a Boost
Volunteer together or cooperate to do an activity that benefits others. Instead of a fancy fundraiser or gala, think beyond just writing a check. There are numerous opportunities that will also help you see your date in a new way. Volunteer for your local homeless shelter? Serve a meal at a soup kitchen?

Agreeing on a cause to support, and how, can give you a glimpse of your future. Being in a community together, even if it's just for an hour, is good practice.

Kindness and generosity are attractive. Also, seeing how your date behaves when it comes to helping others is important. If they work at half-steam, are rude to the people they're supposed to be supporting, lose interest, or give up before the job is done, you've just learned something important about their character. So much of dating (and marriage, and parenthood!) is giving with an open heart and a generous spirit, without any expectation. Can your date do this, or is everything a transaction for them?

Fly Me to The Moon
A tried-and-true date that will help you get to know your partner is a trip out of town, to a place with which neither of you is familiar. Traveling together is a great way to see how compatible you are, even if you aren't going any farther than a four-star luxury hotel in the Hudson Valley. An hour in the car together should tell you plenty about whether or not this person is going to drive you crazy. Do they insist on listening to their favorite music, without asking you your preference? Are they a backseat driver? Do

they put on an eye mask and fall asleep? Once you arrive at your destination, planning how you'll spend your time together will be revealing as well. Shopping trip, or sex all day; turning on the TV or a long walk in the country. When you *can* do anything you want, what you *choose* to do will teach you more about yourself as a couple.

Get away from familiar sights and sounds, out of your usual routine. Even a little inconvenience is worth it if you get a good idea of the person you're dating. Trips can be ultra-romantic—or a total disaster. If something goes wrong, can your date laugh it off? Are they controlling or do they fly by the seat of their pants? Most importantly, are you compatible—or a square peg in a round hole? Worst case scenario, you walk away knowing they were *definitely* not the one. Best case? You bring your girlfriends souvenirs from your week in Dubai and tell them all about the fun you had shopping, skiing, and kissing under the stars.

Take on The World Together
One person's idea of "roughing it" is camping in the rain for a few days. Not glamping, *camping* in a tent. No beds, no bathroom, no hot water, and no food that isn't canned! Another person may think "roughing it" is staying in a two-star hotel with no room service. It's all individual. Now, you shouldn't have to go into full-on survival mode to have a date like this. Maybe a hike together, going on a picnic, or planning a party together will show you how you work together.

Even the most sheltered man who's never even held a hammer in his life has a secret desire to be a manly man in your eyes. It's sexy when guys get down to their instinctive selves. If you go on a hike, you encounter things that might be a little scary. Depending where you go, your hike might be long or steep. You might see wild animals. You never know how someone will feel in unfamiliar territory. Does he act like a man, or hide behind you?

Experiences bond a person. When you encounter danger, does your date stay calm or panic? Going out on a limb together is all about facing your fear of the unknown. That's something you see when you travel together, and one of you has a fear of flying. How do they respond to your fear? Do they nurture you, or do they tease you? Bear in mind that men worth keeping are supposed to be protective over you: a woman should be protected on every level. He shouldn't be pretending that the plane is going to crash or making fun of you!

My Big Fat Family Drama

Dr. Gluck: As we said, marriage is about family. When you partner with someone, become committed, and marry, you're building a new kind of family. The difference between your marriage and your biological family is that your romantic relationship is a family of choice. You are selecting someone to join you in your life together—and that includes your family of origin, too. When you date someone seriously, include them in your family events and plan on attending theirs as well. The more serious you are, the earlier you can introduce your date to your family.

Rori: Look, I don't care if you only see your family at weddings and funerals. When you think you met someone worthwhile, you introduce them to your family. Meeting the parents, especially, is a big deal. You're building a life with this new person. You've got to make sure everyone gets along or can at least be on their best behavior. Family is family. You may not get along with yours, but I can guarantee you that they aren't going anywhere.

Family relationships are another test for your growing relationship. Some people totally revert to adolescence when they're around their parents. Forty-year-old guys act like teenagers at home, put their feet on the sofa, and sneak chips before dinner. Other men expect to be waited on by their mothers. I say, if you want to see what someone's expectations are for you, go home with them and have dinner with their family. I don't care how mature and enlightened a man is. If his mom is a very traditional, domestic goddess type, that's part of how he understands what "wife" means.

Dr. Gluck: Family and formative experiences are enormously influential on the developing brain. We have a pop psychology understanding of Freud, sure, but all therapy takes into account that our relationships with our parents, siblings, and all other family members form the lens through which we see the world. Although the individual may work on issues that developed from those early experiences, they are influenced and shaped by them for the duration of their lives. Now, that's not meant to sound depressing. Most people turn out okay, even those with difficult childhoods or some family dysfunction.

How a person relates to their family and how they conceive of their role within the family is important to you, if you're entering into a commitment. It's been said that "when you marry somebody, you marry the family." That's true, to varying degrees. Some people spend every weekend with their family, plan group vacations and parties, and get together as often as possible. Others are estranged or gather only once a year for a reunion. Most importantly, don't try to change family relationships or show up with the idea that you'll be able to "fix" your partner's family.

Rori: That's a great way to make yourself crazy *and* alienate the whole group. Listening to your partner explain why he no longer speaks to his brother is one thing. Running into that same brother at the summer barbecue and trying to mend those fences, is another. The good news is, when you date as an adult, you should both have more mature relationships with your family members than you did in college. You're not twenty-one anymore! Later in life, especially when you've already gotten through your first marriage and divorce, families tend to be a little more mellow.

Of course, that doesn't mean you shouldn't take family seriously. I think it's attractive when someone has a good connection with their parents. I like to see a guy's father treat him like a man, not a little boy. I like to see the support and the love. It's a peek into your partner's past and also one into your potential future together.

Dr. Gluck: Every family is distinct. In the family department, look for the similarities, not the differences. Your family may not socialize in the same way as your partner's. Focus on values. What does this family care about, and how has your partner adopted those values? Unless you're dating someone who's a real black sheep, there will be a connection.

Now, there are exceptions. If your partner is of a very different background—whether it's race, class, culture, or religion—be prepared for a rocky experience. You may not understand your partner's family. Try to keep an open mind and don't step on anyone's toes. If you're not Jewish, for example, but you were invited to the family Seder dinner, read up on Jewish traditions and prepare yourself. That's good manners, and it's also a way of showing respect. If you're asked to join in a family tradition, such as decorating the Christmas tree or going out to shoot skeet, that's a sign that you're being accepted.

Rori: It's a test, too. Every one of those things is a test. Your partner may love you, but their family needs to accept you, too. I know we're all supposed to be so independent and enlightened these days, but I can't think of any relationship that continued to thrive after it faced serious family disapproval. Like I said, you're not twenty-one any more. It's not romantic to defy your parents and run off to Cabo to get married. Grow up! Your partner's family doesn't *have* to love you, but it sure doesn't hurt.

Don't be shy about adding family to the mix early. Ideally, do this while you're still in the honeymoon period. When you're absolutely nuts about each other, you're excited about the relationship. That's contagious. If you're smitten about your girlfriend, but your mother is down her neck as soon as you walk in the door, that might temper your attraction.

Dr. Gluck: For mature people who are returning to dating after divorce, children are in the "family" category, too. Introducing your children to your partner is a different level of intimacy than introducing your parents.

Rori: When you add your kids, you know it's serious. Family has known you since you were born. They can handle your breakups. Kids, at least the younger ones, get attached. So tread with care. With your older relatives, like your parents, you can bring your new date over in the first three months. With children, you need to wait. Until you really know that the relationship can go the distance, you have no business introducing your children.

The most precious jewels you'll ever have around your neck are the arms of your children. Don't give that up for anything.

Dr. Gluck: If you're dating with marriage in mind, and you have younger school-age children at home, you will want to wait at least six months before you announce that you're in a serious relationship. It's fine for your children to see you going out with your "new friend." However, I'd discourage sleepovers when the children are with you, or fun activities, until you're absolutely certain that your new partner is going to be a permanent part of your life.

Children who have already been through a divorce with you are just as emotionally fragile as you are. You can protect them from disappointment and heartache by keeping your dating life private. Of course, after that, you will want to spend time together "as a family" so that you can see how your partner treats your children, and whether they will accept this new person into their lives.

Rori: First, you have to be patient with your kids. You don't introduce them to their "potential new step parent" on the third date. No. You will regret it. Second, you have to be patient with your partner and find out whether they're worth keeping around. As a parent, your kids must come first. You don't want to hurt them by bringing a new person into their lives every other month, getting them all excited about that person, and then taking that relationship away. It's cruel. I know adults who are still coping with the fact that their mothers had a steady stream of unreliable boyfriends, or their fathers couldn't seem to settle down and kept getting married to woman after woman.

Your choices affect your children. I don't care if your new man makes your heart skip a beat. If you're thinking of marrying him, you're choosing a husband who will be in your home, with your children, every day. If he's verbally abusive or physically rough with your kids, you cannot keep seeing him. *Period*. Remember, husbands are temporary: your children are with you for life. If your kids are older, in college, or all grown up, this isn't such a touchy thing. But for little kids? You need a partner who's caring and safe. Romance is well and good, but there's more to love when it comes to family.

Look, you want a man who is excited to be a stepdad, not someone who sees your children as a liability or a trade-off. If he *ever* gives off the vibe that he'd like you better if you weren't a parent, or he puts up with your kids because he "loves you so much," kick him to the curb. And don't think that having a baby with him will change his mind! You were a parent before you met him, and you'll be a parent when he's gone.

When you commit without compromise, you will have a partner who fits in with your family. Who *feels* like family? Who wants to *be* family?

Dr. Gluck: Family is a fact of life. We call dating the "audition" because it's a long process of deciding whether someone is right for the role of your partner—for life.

Family is part of that role. Why settle for someone who only checks one or two boxes, when you could have someone who fulfills all of them?

The Friend Zone and Fuck-buddies

Rori: Let's talk about the Friend Zone.

Dr. Gluck: The dreaded Friend Zone!

Rori: The Friend Zone is not the same as the place where you put your fuck-buddies. The Friend Zone is what you call the area of your life where you keep people of the opposite sex who aren't ever going to be more than friends.

Dr. Gluck: The Friend Zone is platonic yet can be warm and emotional. These are not acquaintances. These are people with whom you form bonds that have defined boundaries. Your boundaries don't take away from the warmth and fun that comes along with finding true friends and certainly doesn't present any threat to your significant other. Sometimes, these are flirting friends or work colleagues. The Friend Zone can also include people with whom you went on one or two dates and who you like, but don't have any romantic interest.

Rori: Sometimes it becomes really clear that you're better off as friends. This can happen early on, or even after you've gone farther than a few dates. The key here is to always keep your intentions clear and be honest about your feelings. Ask for what you want. Another date? Ask for it. A kiss? Ask for it. A long, sexy night together? Ask for it. Make sure you're on the same page with your attraction. If you're starting to catch feelings, make it obvious, and ask the other person if they feel the same way, too.

If your date's answer to any of these questions is "no," or "not now," decide if you want to be friends instead. You're both adults! You can make these choices. If you like the person's company but don't feel totally compatible, you can either move on or you can stick them in the Friend Zone. It's not an easy decision. You'll have to be firm about putting your needs first, to avoid getting stuck in a relationship that's going nowhere.

Dr. Gluck: Bear in mind that the Friend Zone should be a final decision. Once you've come to the conclusion that this date is a "no," have a polite, in-person conversation with the other person. Make it clear that it's not them: it's just not a fit, romantically. The Friend Zone is not a place to meet new romantic partners. It's cruel to put someone in there, and then change your mind and pull them out again, only to say "no" again down the line.

Be certain when you make this decision. It will help you avoid power plays and non-relationships that suck your energy and time but will never lead you to your goal of happy, married life.

Rori: That's so true. Just like with casual dating, you don't sleep with someone for a year and expect it to somehow add up to a real relationship. Where's the intention? Where's the romance? Following someone around who's not really open to commitment is sad. It will break your heart. The person who's normally in the Friend Zone but still sleeping over every night isn't your boyfriend. They're an FWB: friend with benefits.

Dr. Gluck: That sounds like a fuck-buddy.

Rori: They're not the same thing!

Dr. Gluck: The end result is the same. They might as well be.

Rori: They're not, though. A fuck-buddy is just someone you get off with. There's no connection. It may as well be a one-night stand. The FWB relationship is different because it is problematic. You're basically trading a healthy, fully committed relationship for available sex. There's nothing wrong with that—as long as you're not thinking, in the back of your mind, that this is going to end up in a fairy tale wedding of your dreams. Dream on! Like I said, flirt with whoever you want. Play the field if you're on the rebound. But don't waste your time on a FWB if you're really hoping to get married.

Dr. Gluck: Both men and women who struggle with insecurity and fear of rejection can fall into the FWB habit. It seems to make sense: you have someone to sleep with, no strings attached, while you go on dates in search of a real partner.

Rori: How do people not see the problem with that?

Dr. Gluck: Well, the situation usually comes to a head. There are a few outcomes that we see, over and over. One, the FWB develops an emotional attachment. Suddenly, you're not dealing with a "no strings" arrangement. You've inadvertently created a pseudo-relationship that provides about 20 percent of what you want. You will need to break it off with your buddy, which can feel like a romantic breakup *and* a platonic breakup, at the same time.

Two, you meet someone you want to see seriously and you need to tell the FWB you're moving on. That hurts people's feelings and can create intense jealousy. I know few people who would be fine with learning that, while you're wining and dining them, you're sleeping next to someone else and getting physically intimate with *them*. Your date may also be turned off by your willingness to live a double life: it points to cheating in the future, because you're comfortable sitting across your date for a romantic dinner, while screwing your FWB or keeping a fuck-buddy on the sly. You can create trust by staying focused on *one* person: the person you might want to be with, for the long run.

Three, you develop an attachment to your FWB, but they don't reciprocate, or aren't able to offer you a relationship of the caliber you want. You have to move on for your sanity. You'd be surprised how long this can take. It's usually not an overnight change. Because you've been casual with the pseudo-relationship, the breakup may not feel final. It's easy to slip back into your old habits and patterns, because they're easy. The minimal payoff in this situation is the bait that keeps you going back for more—to your detriment.

Rori: Either way, you just wasted your time. Keep it in your pants until you meet someone worth sleeping with. FWBs are fun when you're not looking for the real deal, but you can't have a side piece and expect everything to work out smoothly.

Don't have a fuck-buddy, and don't *be* a fuck-buddy. Keep your friendships friendly, not frisky. When you're serious about love, make it known. Your convictions will cause the people who don't align with your ideals to leave your life.

The same is true for the Friend Zone: if you say "no, thanks" to someone who's not thrilled about staying platonic, they'll show themselves the door. Your job is to keep your eyes on the prize and maintain healthy boundaries. Put yourself first and the rest will follow.

Relationships are a learning experience. You learn about yourself. You learn about the other person. And you do the work to learn about yourselves as a couple.

Chapter 8

Avoiding Pitfalls and Tiger Traps

The Art of the Date uses the Platinum Poire method to help you find a relationship that works for *you*. Everyone is different, which is why we avoid hard rules, negative talk, or focusing on limitations. On your way to Happily Ever After, we suggest a few guidelines that can help you avoid disasters.

Many people find that, as they fall in love, they lose perspective of their own relationship. They don't see the pitfalls because they're in love! It can be hard to tell which way is up when that special someone kisses you. In every transition of the love cycle, there's a need for a new perspective, philosophy, and communication. These changes are necessary if you are going to develop into a successful couple.

Learning to read the red flags in a relationship will save you a heartbreak. The best part is, the pitfalls you may encounter are based in your own boundaries, expectations, and needs—which means *you* are the person who's best equipped to handle relationship problems when they come up.

In this chapter, Rori and Dr. Gluck will share their insights to help you define deal breakers and enforce boundaries, even when you're falling head over heels. By avoiding the pitfalls of dating and identifying tiger traps, you will be able to find a match that isn't going to let you down or blow up in your face.

Love the Player, Hate the Game

Dr. Gluck: One of the major pitfalls of dating is the player: the charming, fun person, usually a man, who is very romantic but avoids any kind of commitment.

Rori: "Player" is a nice way of saying he's a liar.

Dr. Gluck: Whoever loves least in the relationship has the most power. That's what a player is doing. He causes his partner to form an emotional attachment without reciprocating.

Rori: But he lies about it! He says all those sweet things that really get her purring. He sends gifts, takes her on romantic getaways, and spends all night making her toes curl. What she doesn't know is that he's doing the same thing with six other women, and *they* all think he's their boyfriend, too. The lying is the problem here, and that's what sets his guy apart from your standard-issue short-term schmuck. It's one thing to have a fling. You should go into it with your eyes open. The player takes that choice away, because he doesn't seem to treat the fun and sex and dating like a fling. It is to him, but it won't feel that way to his victim.

Dr. Gluck: Honestly, I think some women prefer to date players. They fool themselves into thinking they're the only one in his life. There's the challenge of changing him or making him fall in love. They want to change him.

Rori: They are going to end up with a broken heart and an STD. Love can't be one-sided, and players are so emotionally detached that they get very manipulative. With men like this, it's all about the challenge and "getting" a woman. It's all about the *get*. Once they've got her, they're like, *whatever*. They move on to the next woman, sometimes without telling the first one that she's old news.

Dr. Gluck: The only way to break that cycle is to leave. Between jealousy, sexual attraction, and dishonesty, a relationship with a player is guaranteed to make you crazy.

Rori: Some women like that! If the man's challenge is to "get" the woman, the woman's challenge is to "tame" the man. So many rom-coms have that same story, and it always works out. Well, this is not Hollywood: it's New York. Get a grip.

Once you figure out that a guy is playing you, have some self-respect and walk away. He's not going to commit to you. He's not going to settle. Sticking around is just going to make things worse. Guys like this are so smooth, it can be hard to spot what they're doing until it's too late. The next thing you know, you're humiliated and you've lost your faith in love. Don't do that to yourself.

Dr. Gluck: Once bitten, twice shy. A good guy will be open about his intentions and whether or not he's seeing other people. The problem with players isn't that they play you. The experience may also set you up to be more vulnerable in the future, or even miss out on a healthy connection later. A bad run-in with a player can give you trust issues that affect your next relationship—or next *several* relationships. Do your future self a favor and pass on players. You may think you can handle it, but most people become very unhappy once it's clear that the "relationship" isn't real.

Rori: Reputations are sexually transmitted, too. If you get a reputation for running around with players, or people think you're a fool or naive, that's not going to go away quickly. Listen to your gut and do *not* go back for seconds.

From Here to Eternity, Or Just Next Week?

Dr. Gluck: One of the biggest decisions we see people making is how long of a relationship they're looking for. Is this for now, or for life? Some couples are looking for short-term dating, of a year or more. Others seek something that will last for at least the next ten years. Others only want a partner they could be married to for life.

The element of time applies in the bigger picture, as well as the day to day of dating. If you are seeing a potential partner, and they're not interested in a lifelong commitment, don't try to convince them to change their mind. You can assume that they're being honest with you, not playing hard to get. Rather than convert your date to your way of thinking, let them go and look for someone whose relationship goals match their own.

Rori: Marriage is like any other negotiation. If the two parties don't see eye to eye about the terms of the agreement, it's not going to work. Also, if they don't bring equal interest to the table, that won't work either. Instead of thinking that your partner's deep, romantic streak is somehow going to make you feel differently about love, be real with yourself. Are you a committer, or a quitter? If you're really only interested in a girlfriend who will be around for a couple years, then you need to say so. Don't string her along, thinking she's going to get a ring on her

141

finger and a big family wedding. You'll make each other miserable. Women are like stock. Once the age starts going up, the options start going down.

If your potential partner's goals aren't the same as yours, that's not a moral thing. It just means you're not a match. No judgment from me: honesty is what's important.

Dr. Gluck: This is why unconventional relationships, such as sugar babies and sugar daddies, sometimes work out for the best. We don't judge the people who enter into these arrangements. In some ways, we can learn from them. In these matches, both parties are completely transparent about what they want. Companionship or intimacy is exchanged for financial security. Each partner has clear expectations about what they're getting from the relationship. They both understand there's an expiration date.

When you think of your current dating situation, or the relationship you'd like to be in, it's necessary to be clear about your own ability to establish and keep a timeframe. Remember, brutal honesty prevents brutal fights. Especially if there's an age discrepancy, it's important that there's a clear understanding of the commitments that you are making, as well as your partners. Anything swept under the carpet will lead to emotional and intimate problems that will find their way from your communication into the bedroom.

Be respectful of your own time and theirs. Is time something that you discuss with your potential partner? Perhaps, when you were a young college student, you had time to "find yourself" and experiment more with relationships. As an older, wiser person you may feel differently about time. Back then, a year was a long time. Now, it's nothing at all.

Rori: It's so tempting to "keep it open." You meet someone, you like them, you want to date them, and then, instead of committing, you say you'll "keep it open." That's the worst idea. People who "keep it open" don't close relationships. They're the ones looking for the ring box under the Christmas tree, year after year. Be up front about what you're able to give, in terms of time, and if it's not a fit, move on to someone who is. Don't break your own heart by trying to seem cool. If you truly want to be married within two years, you have to say so. Otherwise, how is your potential partner going to know what to do with you?

Many women feel insecure about time. They want their man to put a ring on it, but they would never come out and say that. They drop hints, and act like "wife material," but the desire isn't explicit. Their boyfriends love the special treatment and the attention, but that agreement to "keep it open" is their loophole. Unless your man is a *man* and he's eager to commit, I guarantee you that he will drag not only his feet, but your heart too, every step of the way. The woman might even end up proposing to him, out of desperation!

When a woman sets the tone in a relationship early on that she is the hunter or the aggressor, she's going to be disappointed. She is going to wake up one day and ask, "Where is my man?" Honey, you emasculated him. You have to make up your mind: do you want to be the man or woman in the relationship? Be honest with yourself. Taking the offensive and chasing him down is just not sexy. You can't be the man *and* the woman in the relationship and expect it to work out.

A girlfriend of mine was very bossy and pushy with her guy. They were staying at her place one night and she heard a noise in the kitchen. It sounded like somebody was trying to break in. She turned to her boyfriend and said, "Aren't you going to go check it out?" He was hiding under the covers! Hiding behind her!

"You first," he said. Let's just say, it didn't last much longer.

Talk Monogamy to Me, Baby

Platinum Poire matches work because the expectations are very clear for everyone in the relationship. We interview our clients about their desires, the length of their ideal relationship, and what they can offer a partner. I think that's very romantic, because it gives the gift of stability, right from the beginning of the relationship. If you're both looking for marriage, why settle for less? Putting it on the table, right from the beginning, helps you avoid players and fly-by-night types. All you have to do is say the "M word" and they'll run right out the door!

Dr. Gluck: When you and your potential partner share a relationship goal, and you're on the same "schedule," the chances of staying together increase. You have a good chance of staying together. Timelines can make a couple feel like they're really working together to create a shared future. For example, if you both agree that you would like to date for a year, then get engaged, and be pregnant by the time the second anniversary rolls around, you've got that timeline in common. Even if you don't end up engaged, and part ways before the first year is up, you were both true to your timelines. You started that relationships with certain agreed upon rules and goals. Rules are how you get there, goals are what you would like to reach. A mutual agreement to date in a certain way, with clearly defined milestones. Does this kill the romance? No. Defining goals gives you the opportunity to really open up to one another.

Rori: If you don't ask, you don't get. Instead of playing coy and saying you'll "just see what happens," respect your time and your potential partner. For example, if your date is really eager to have more children, and she's close to forty, time is going to be an issue. This goes for the guys, too: maybe *he* wants kids, while he feels healthy enough to play football with them. Put those asks on the table and be up-front. Again, this is a basic question that will screen out people who just aren't a match.

It's also smart to have those milestones clearly established because it gives you a deadline. Is that harsh? I don't think so. If you said, very clearly, that you wanted to be engaged by the end of your first year together, and there is still no ring, you can step back and assess the situation. Is your boyfriend messing with you? Does he take the relationship seriously? Or is something else going on? When you put that year on the table, you're defining your expectations and, if necessary, leave with your dignity intact. No ring, no relationship.

Dr. Gluck: The "M word" scares people. Even those who have been married before can feel some fear around marriage and what it means. Grief counseling can help someone process their divorce, get in better shape mentally, and become open to a new partnership. No matter what, fear of commitment shouldn't be a limitation in the relationship. If your date brings up marriage, and you flinch, this is a signal that you need to go deeper in examining the pros and cons of the relationship. When the relationship is right, it should feel peaceful. That is probably a signal that you shouldn't be dating seriously—or at least, not dating *her*.

Rori: Shared goals and a timeline for your commitment are one way to avoid relationships that don't seem to go anywhere. It's possible to share these goals without turning the pressure up. You don't have to be crazy about it! Instead of turning it on the other person and asking questions like, "Where do you see this going?" you can talk about *your* desired outcome. You can say, in a clear and mature way, "This is what I'm looking for, and this is the time frame with which I'm working." You can negotiate to get what you want.

The right person will resonate with your goals and be excited to share their own as well.

Dr. Gluck: Depending on how seriously you consider time a factor in your relationship, you might even follow a business-style approach to dating. This means creating very clear expectations, including check-ins and reviews. Remember that your first date is the audition. If you both pass, you can move into a quarterly system: every three or four months you have a sit-down, to analyze the strengths and weaknesses of the relationship. Now, some people really like this format, and others don't get much out of it. It depends on what kind of couple you are.

I suggest that, whether you're checking in over cocktails and tapas or on the couch with a relationship counselor, you must make time to have those big conversations. If you're both part of a particular faith tradition, you may want to meet with your pastor or rabbi (or whatever religious or spiritual figure) about premarital counseling as well. As always, if you find yourself *not* wanting to attend those meetings or have those conversations, that's a sign that this is not the relationship for you.

Rori: At any time, you can raise the stakes of the relationship by going back to your timeline. It takes a year to plan a wedding. It takes nine months to have a baby, and some people don't get pregnant on the first try. You have to consider time when you say you want these things. Most of all, keep in mind that life very rarely goes according to plan. You can commit to a timeline, but you can't control how life unfolds. I love that quote: "Man plans, God laughs." It's true! The point here isn't that you and your potential partner agree on a five-year plan and then execute it perfectly. It means that you're able to talk honestly about your goals and expectations and figure out whether you're on the same page. The important thing is coming to those agreements together. How life turns out is anyone's guess.

Weddings Are the Reason for the Season

Rori: I love weddings! There's a time in life when everyone's friends and relatives and cousins all seem to get married at once. I'm talking, a dozen weddings in one summer. When you're in a committed relationship, the person you're dating is probably going to get invited along, too.

Dr. Gluck: Weddings are a cultural intersection of many different, important elements of life. Love, commitment, family, community, money, faith, children, all of it is tied up in this one ceremony. Even though each wedding can be as diverse as the couple getting married, those essential elements don't change. When you bring a partner to the wedding, you're exposing them to a larger part of your community and your life.

Attending a wedding together naturally opens up the question, "Will this be something we do, too? When?" With a couple that's already talked about marriage, weddings are probably not a huge deal. It's a question that's been settled. You might daydream about your wedding, even if you're not already engaged. It's not an intimidating subject. For couples who haven't broached the subject yet, weddings can be tough. The way your partner behaves at a wedding, and whether they're willing to talk about the future you might share, tells you plenty about their goals for the relationship. Romance is fantasy: everyone enjoys it. Weddings are real, and not everyone is capable of connecting their daydreams with their reality.

You're also going to see people at weddings who you may not see all the time. The extended family, especially, is a part of many weddings. You may be asked— or told—many times that "You're next!" A bride may hand off her garter or bouquet deliberately. How your partner handles this light-hearted teasing is very telling. If they seem resentful, that tells you that they're not emotionally ready to make a commitment at the same level.

Rori: I think weddings are so romantic and fun. If you're the guest, you eat a good meal, drink a little, dance, and have a great time. They're always super positive events, with people coming together to celebrate love. What's not to like? For me, it would be a red flag if I took my partner to a wedding and they somehow manage to have a terrible time. The worst thing is to go to a wedding where you don't believe a couple will make it past the honeymoon. You don't want to be a Negative Nancy, it's but really hard to be there if you don't believe in the situation. A good marriage is one that everyone celebrates. Who wants to tie the knot if the whole world thinks you're a disaster waiting to happen?

I think that, when you see your partner in different situations, you learn more about them. A wedding is one of those things that you end up doing as a couple. If a man can handle whitewater rafting or whatever, but the idea of dancing with one of your aunts terrifies him, that's something at which you may want to take a closer look. Some people, men especially, want the marriage but not the wedding. They want the commitment without the community. Sometimes guys don't want to worry about the flowers and other decisions. They just want it to get done.

If that's how he's thinking, he's got another thought coming. There are no shortcuts in love. If you can't agree, or if his vision of your future doesn't match yours, he's not your man.

Dr. Gluck: Wedding season is partially about endurance, too. Going to three, four, or ten weddings in a row means you're giving up every summer weekend. Does your potential partner complain about this, or look forward to it? If you're in the wedding party, do they support you?

Are they on their best behavior at the wedding, or do they have too much to drink and roast the groom? Wedding season is a test of any relationship, especially where there hasn't been a formal commitment yet. Ideally, you leave wedding season with renewed excitement for your own relationship, and a clear vision of your future together.

Platinum Qualities Enrich Your Love

Rori: In a platinum relationship, you never settle for less than what you desire and deserve. You don't commit to a relationship that's less than the best. You're worth it. The relationship that lasts decades and enriches your life in every way is not just built on financial compatibility, shared goals, and good communication. There's another level, underneath the stuff you encounter on the surface.

Dr. Gluck: The qualities you want in a long-term partnership used to be called *virtues*. That's an old-fashioned word. Now, we call them ideals or character traits. Everyone has some of these positive traits, to some degree. Some people have more than others, due to their family backgrounds, interests, life experiences, and personal convictions. In my career as a profiler, I've observed many kinds of people. They usually have the same qualities in varying amounts: one person may be extremely honest, but lack stamina for hard conversations. Another one may have plenty of ambition but come up a little short in the compassion category. Again, nobody is perfect, but *somebody* is going to be perfect for *you*.

Before you look for a partner with a certain personality, analyze yourself. What are your strengths? What are your weaknesses? A healthy relationship will bring out the best in you, and your ideal partner has a personality that complements yours. Remember that you're a fully formed, mature person: you don't need anyone to "complete" you.

Rori: At Platinum Poire, we rely on interviews and in-person experiences to determine whether you're a match. Algorithms and personality tests can't show how magical it feels to be with you or describe what it's like to go one a date with you. When you're using our method, you'll learn things about your partner *over time*. You can create opportunities to see their personality clearly and learn about their values. You have to put in the work to discover who they really are. Those essential personality traits *will* come out. Sometimes, it's inspiring. Other times, terrifying! You might wonder, where on earth is this coming from?

When someone shows you who they are, believe them. You can't change someone's values to suit you. They're not a custom Porsche, with all the bells and whistles you want. People show up as themselves. You need to take time to learn what they're really made of and then decide if that's going to work for you or not. You never have to settle for less.

Dr. Gluck: With patience, you can also find out where the person's values come from. Maybe their father always emphasized loyalty as being important, so they acquired that value from him. Their experience causes them to place a higher priority on that particular value, and they won't be drawn to people who don't feel the same. Or maybe they had a bad experience, where someone broke their trust, and now honesty is high on the priority list.

The platinum values you share with your potential partner determine at every step whether you want to continue. What are the values that matter to you? What are the platinum qualities of this person you're dating? Here are some questions that will help you determine what your values are, and help you learn more about what your partner cares about:

> I want other people to think of me as
  _____.

> My biggest asset is _____.

> I could never date someone who doesn't have as much _____ as I do because _____.

> In my family, _____ is the most important value.

> To me, integrity means _____.

> The worst thing anyone could ever do is
  _____.

> In my ideal relationship, my partner is
  _____.

Growing Together Means Growing a Pair

Rori: Look, we may live in a more enlightened society, where men and women mix differently than we did one hundred years ago, but the fact is that romance changes your existing relationships too. When you commit to someone, it means that your other relationships are probably going to evolve as well. You can embrace this, or you can fight it, but either way, it's part of commitment.

Dr. Gluck: Your partner's jealousy must be taken into account, of course. If you've been very flirtatious with certain people, that's a behavior that will probably change. Close friendships with people of the opposite sex, or people you formerly had a sexual relationship with, will also change. There's nothing wrong with keeping these friends in your life. However, in a committed relationship, you will end up making decisions. Some friends will be with you forever, no matter to whom you're married. Others will have new roles in your life.

Now, in the ideal relationship, you will never have to choose between your partner and your friends.

Rori: That's right. The person who loves you, loves the people you love.

Dr. Gluck: Love should be freeing. If the key fits the lock, it's effortless. The right key shouldn't be jamming and should always open the door.

Rori: You should also protect your relationship. If you go to lunch every week with your besties and they continually trash your partner, what are they really saying about you? If your partner feels uncomfortable around certain friends, or is not included at parties, you need to take action or you are going to lose your relationship. When you make a commitment to a partner, you will need to assess your social circle. Decide who stays, who's not allowed to be around your partner, and who to cut off. Listen to your heart.

Dr. Gluck: Listen to your friends, too. Maybe they say negative things, but if they are *all* saying the same things, that's a red flag. Do they see something you don't? Do they feel this person isn't deserving of your time?

Rori: The person you commit to is going to take up a large slice of your life. That's the point! You'll share a home together, raise children, have your own family. That is precious. You need to honor your partner by acknowledging their role in your life. That doesn't mean completely ditching all your friends. Hell to the no! That's so codependent. What you can do is notice how your friends treat your partner.

Most people will be very warm and welcoming. They want to make your new partner feel like they're part of the group. They'll respect that you love this person. They get it.

Other people are going to be a problem. You can avoid a major tiger trap and many of awkward moments by dealing with this dynamic early on.

Dr. Gluck: Changing relationship dynamics is something that happens naturally, throughout the span of human life. People come and go. Some people keep friends forever: they grew up on the same block, played on the same baseball team, and still see each other twice a week for happy hour. Other people have fluid relationships and find new friend groups every few years. Shared values, community activities, and availability dictate whether someone will stay connected to a group of friends.

In a partnership, each person comes with a group of friends and relationships that meet different needs. They have many groups with whom they connect. These are connections that you keep. In a romantic relationship, spending time together one-on-one should always be the priority. If you can't enjoy the one-to-one, you are in the wrong relationship. There should be a level of trust to grow your relationship with your partner's friends in a way that doesn't take away from that need for separate time, alone.

The more you're connected to people, the more sane you're going to stay.

Rori: I would say that one of those "shared values" is respect. I would have a hard time staying with a guy whose friends were rude to me every time I saw them. I think it would be tough on the romantic relationship and hard on his friendships also. Like, why would he throw me in the shark tank like that? In a partnership, your partner is half of you. They're going to see your friends at work functions, fundraisers, weekend parties—they'll be there. You never want to be in that situation where you come to a point of "it's me or them." Nothing is worse. It's also really crappy if your friends are disrespectful toward your partner. Like, what does that say about you? If your friends don't treat your partner kindly, even as a favor to your friendship, what kind of friends are they?

Dr. Gluck: Ideally, you avoid ultimatums with some foresight. In some cases, it means simply accepting that there will be some level of conflict. You may have "boys' nights" with your friends instead of double- or triple-dates with your friends and their partners. You may also revisit your boundaries with your friends. In mature friendships, it's perfectly acceptable to stand up for your partner. You can say, "It hurts me when you talk about my partner that way. Please be respectful, even if you don't like her."

Rori: A man will always make his girlfriend or wife feel respected, protected, and cared for. He doesn't subject her to situations that make her feel small, disrespected, or unwelcome. That's not okay. The woman who you choose

155

as your partner, especially if she's your wife, deserves your utmost respect. There should be no locker room talk about her. You don't tell your buddies things that would make her seem less in their eyes. What kind of man does that? A guy who makes fun of his partner with his friends isn't a man. This is what separates the men from the boys.

The same thing with the ladies. It's one thing to dish about every little dirty detail of a one-night stand. Your boy toy couldn't get it up? He fell asleep in the middle of things? That's funny. But you would think twice before sharing the same story about your husband. Why? Because your husband *knows* your friends. He spends time with them, at the same parties and gatherings. When you overshare about your sex life, you expose your husband to ridicule. You hurt his reputation. Keep your mouth shut about his shortcomings, or you risk undermining your relationship.

People's values and ideals come from our community. It's like a second family: there are expectations about how you'll spend your time with your partner's friends. For some couples, it's a no-brainer: they do everything together. Maybe they were friends or acquaintances before they started dating—that simplifies things, in the friend department. Other couples prefer to keep their friend groups separate, and don't go to every social event together. You have to figure out what works for you. I can tell you, though, that one bad experience can really cause problems in your relationship.

How your friends talk about and treat your partner is revealing. Even if they don't love-love-love the person you're dating, they should at least be polite! Whether it's your first husband or your fifth, good friends support you through it all.

Dr. Gluck: The ones who don't, are not good friends. As time goes on, and you observe how your social circle behaves with your partner, you'll learn who has your best interests at heart. Having those hard conversations with your friends isn't easy, but it's necessary. You may also be pleasantly surprised. Rather than breaking off a friendship or severely limiting your contact with a friend, you may open new understanding with them. After all, friends feel jealous too.

Everyone speaks a different language. Your friends may not speak the same language as your partner. It's a perfect time to enlighten them, rather than fight.

Rori: That's a different kind of jealousy. The question is, are you going to deal with it, or let it ruin your life? Consider your partner. Would they be happy with the way you're describing them to your friends? Do they fit in with your crowd, or should you plan to go alone?

Honestly, refusing to address issues in your friend group or with your partner is pretty much guaranteed to create those pitfalls that destroy relationships. If you think ahead, listen to your heart, make decisions based on your principles, and speak honestly, you will be able to sidestep most problems. If you avoid them—you have no one to blame but yourself. Don't undermine your happiness by refusing to look at the bigger picture. You're allowed to have clear expectations for all your relationships. Just make sure your actions match your priorities.

Chapter 9

Baby, You're a Perfect Ten

Why linger in a relationship that's an "eight" when you know you deserve a "ten"? You don't have to settle until you're sure you have found someone who's fully worth your time and energy. If you're dating with the intention of finding a match for life, it pays to be discerning. Although you may worry about finding "The One," focus on finding a "ten" instead. Your soulmate isn't one specific person. It's the person who feels right to you, brings out your best side, and is someone with whom you're excited to spend your days, months, and years.

Now, there's pressure to settle no matter *who* you are. Whether you're a billionaire or flipping burgers, you'll hear the message that "you should take what you can get." You may have some insecurities from past rejections or bad relationships that make you think that braving the dating world isn't something you can handle again. You may not trust your intuition to select a partner that fulfills your needs. The Platinum Poire method is designed to help you understand what your instincts are telling you about a potential match, and to help you decide whether they're a person who belongs in your life—or not.

When you settle, what you're really saying is, "This relationship is more important than my happiness. This is good enough for me because I don't think much of myself."

159

To break through that kind of self-defeating thinking, you need to change your goals and expectations. Absolutely bring your best self to the table—and expect your date to do the same. In this chapter, Rori and Dr. Gluck discuss why settling for something *good* is actually robbing you of having the *best* relationship you can find.

I Love You But, I Love Me More

Dr. Gluck: Your most important relationship is the one you have with yourself. Your ego must be satisfied; your life must be lived. Whether you're deeply committed to another person, or a lifelong bachelor, that's the way it is. This is why Platinum Poire suggests working on yourself before you go searching for the love of your life. You should like yourself, inside and out. If you're not ready when the right person comes along, you risk missing an opportunity of your lifetime. Psychologically, physically, and financially, you should be in good shape.

This isn't a self-serving mission. When you are at your best, you bring your best. You bring out the best in others, too. You work better, have more fun with your friends, and you're a better, more present parent to your children. Everyone benefits—including you. When you bring that energy into searching for a relationship, you are bound to get better results than if you start out at less than your best.

Rori: Albert Einstein said, "Any man who can drive safely while kissing a pretty girl is simply not giving the kiss the attention it deserves." That's the kind of focus you need when you're looking for your soulmate. You don't half-ass it. You give it your all. I promise you, every ounce of energy you invest in this search will come back to you, one hundred times over. Considering that you're looking for someone you'll see every day, at least twice a day, for the rest of your life, that's a really big investment. This is the person with whom you'll sleep, eat, raise children, play, and learn. When you invest that energy and passion into your search, you're not just saying "I'm ready for love." You're also saying, "I love myself enough to treat myself like number one."

When you treat yourself with respect, you attract respect. When you take care of your body, you attract people who do the same. Like attracts like. So often, people are desperate for a relationship, *any* relationship! They never do any work on themselves, and they end up attracting someone who is only providing about 75 percent of what they really need. Or, they stay in these semi-satisfying relationships for years, wishing things would get better. You've got to start with good materials in order to build something of which you're really excited to be a part. Cutting corners and compromise is how you end up unhappy, lonely, and back at square one. Give your attention to those kisses, like Einstein said!

Dr. Gluck: Psychological studies show that you become like the five people who are the closest to you. They influence you in subtle and obvious ways. If your closest friends, family members, and colleagues are not go-getters, you probably aren't either. If your inner circle is very ambitious, or motivated to improve the world, that's contagious too. The truth is, you can change the people with whom you spend time. One of the people in that small group of five influencers will be your partner, so choose them wisely. There are no excuses: the truth is you can choose with whom you spend time.

Now, this relationship doesn't need to be purely aspirational. You can use the questions and exercises in the previous chapters to make sure that your goals match your potential partner. You should enjoy their company. You should have fun with them. You shouldn't choose them because they're going to fix you, complete you, or teach you their ways. Don't date a tall person just because you think it will make your posture better! But do date people who reflect your value back to you. Over the years, your weight will change, your hair will recede, and your material circumstances may be unstable. But your inherent worth should feel enriched by the person with whom you choose to spend your life.

Rori: Don't settle for a relationship that won't let you be yourself. That's the big one, for many of the divorced people I know. They compromised because they chose hot sex, status, or money over their inner worth. It's an easy mistake to make; luckily, you don't have to stay in that relationship for life. Your freedom and happiness are much more important than what your boyfriend drives. With that said, a Maserati in the garage can be an added fun perk!

I'm a Sagittarius, so for me, relationships represent freedom. I feel empowered in my marriage to live my life, dream big, and explore everything the world has to offer. One of the many reasons I'm so happy with my husband now is that he encourages and supports me to test my own limits. He believes in me. He never tries to control me or shut me down—though he does call me out when he knows

I'm being an unreasonable bitch. The freedom I have with him would seem like it's the opposite of a traditional marriage, but that's not the case for me. My experience is that our love and commitment actually fuel my fire. It's always based in that mutual trust and respect. I know who I am, and I've married a man who loves the person I am.

It wasn't always that way. I loved my ex, but I knew he just wasn't for me. I finally had to say to him, "You love me, but you don't like me." I couldn't change him. I knew he loved me but there is so much more to a relationship. I couldn't count on love to solve all our other problems. We throw the word "love" around, but it's much more meaningful to be with someone you *like* and respect.

It's a man's job to respect women, but it's a woman's job to give him something to respect. Don't ever lower your standards for anyone—not your friends, not your husband, and not yourself. Self-respect is everything. When you begin dating, and you're already in love with yourself, you'll find someone else who feels the same way, too. I am confident that my relationship is a "ten" because I met Charles when I was at the top of my game, and so was he. We were drawn to each other not only because we are so compatible, but because we were both at that level. We clicked. If I'd been tripping over my own Manolos, I don't think we could have connected in the same way.

Dr. Gluck: Healthy relationships encourage mutual growth, and they accommodate each person as they grow within the partnership. It's possible that people outgrow each other: college sweethearts aren't always meant to last a lifetime. But I think it's important to point out that not all relationships are forever. Our culture emphasizes longevity as the sign of success in marriage, but I don't think that's accurate. I would take a relationship of five years where I was deliriously happy, every single day, over a relationship that was five times as long but only a fraction as satisfying. Happiness, not length, is how we measure success at Platinum Poire. When both people are happy, they share that happiness. They lead fulfilling lives. They, in turn, enrich the people around them.

Rori: You don't get that kind of happiness by compromising yourself or dating down. If you ever feel like you could do better, guess what? It's because you can, and you should. You should never have that feeling that you're at the wrong party, standing next to the wrong guy. Life's too short for that. You deserve the best, so act like it—and date like it, too.

Dr. Gluck: It is a sign of a healthy ego to put your needs first. Codependent relationships become unhealthy because at least one partner in the relationship is taking the back seat. They may hate their partner's friends but acquiesce because they want to "seem" like a good date. They may enable their partner's drinking habits because they want to avoid conflict and make the relationship "seem" normal. Those are two obvious examples; there are a thousand more subtle ones. Once your needs start coming in second, you're headed for trouble. It's the difference between who you are in your skin and who you are in your clothes. You can change your suit. That, you can change. Your apparel changes. But the leopard can't change its spots, just as you can't compromise on things that are too much of what you are.

It's not about *winning*. It's about being able to hear one another.

Now, I'm not saying that you shouldn't be willing to compromise. Someone needs to take the kids to the dentist. Maybe she knows more about clothes, so you let her pick your ties. Sharing responsibilities in a respectful way shouldn't trample on either of you. Relationships are created through sharing and communicating. Even if you don't get your way in an argument, you should still feel heard. Compromising in a discussion isn't the same as compromising your self-care or your self-respect.

Rori: Repeat after me. "I love you, but I love me more." You have permission to put yourself first, whether you're in a relationship or not. Loving yourself isn't self-centered or selfish. Who else are you going to give that love to? Take care of yourself first, and you'll see improvements in every area of your life. That's definitely true of dating. Who wants to go out with someone who clearly hates their body, job, education, or family? That's so unattractive. People who don't love themselves ooze negativity. They never have anything nice to say. It's always bad talk about the people they know, or grudges they've been dragging around for years. Boring!

Like Dr. Gluck said, that negative stuff is contagious. Do you want someone like that dragging you down? No way! If you are spending time with someone who makes you feel less-than-magical, or whose cynicism puts you in a bad mood for the rest of the day, walk away without regret. Sarcasm is not sexy: it's a turn off. Putting people down isn't sexy, either. Trash talk is not a turn-on. You don't need someone else's garbage in your life. Look, some girls are born with glitter in their veins. Never settle for a man who dulls your sparkle. You're a gem and you deserve a man who sees your worth and treats you like his queen.

Dr. Gluck: If you act like a court jester … you deserve what you get!

Rejection Is God's Protection

Dr. Gluck: Settling is often a response to an earlier, negative experience. You might come out of a bad relationship or a nasty divorce thinking, "Well, my last partner didn't want me, so I should lower my expectations."

Rori: Don't you do that!

Dr. Gluck: The fear is natural, though. It's a feeling through which you can work. The fear of rejection, or being inherently unlovable, is something most of us cope with at one time or another. Why did your relationship end? What is making you feel like you're not enough? Sometimes, talking to a therapist, life coach, or a trusted friend will help you understand that your last breakup wasn't really about your perceived deficiencies. Take some time to heal and see that situation clearly.

If you tried your best in the last relationship and your wife cheated, maybe your understanding of your "best" isn't aligned with your wife's expectations. Cheating should not end a relationship. The only thing that should end relationship is when you realize your values and goals are no longer completely compatible

For example, what if you tried your best in your last marriage, but your spouse cheated. The affair humiliated and hurt you, and it made you feel like maybe you weren't good enough in bed. Otherwise, your spouse would have been satisfied and stayed faithful. That's a natural response, but it's not grounded in reality. The situation was probably much more complex. I can tell you that people don't cheat because the person they've been married to for years is suddenly no good in the bedroom. Your ex's choices aren't a reflection on you. However, you can carry that anxiety into your next serious relationship.

The temptation, in this example, is to choose a partner who puts a low priority on sex, is less experienced than you are, or is the kind of person who will never arouse your jealousy.

Rori: That doesn't sound great to me. Rationalizing, "Yeah, he's not very handsome, and he doesn't give me butterflies, but at least nobody else will want him" is a terrible way to start a relationship.

Dr. Gluck: one man's trash is another man's treasure. The problem is, many people don't realize that their insecurity is causing them to make this decision. They don't see it in a cut-and-dried way. They perceive this new potential partner as someone who doesn't threaten them or make their insecurity worse. It's a cycle that can go on for many relationships, and many years.

Rori: Once you start lowering your expectations, how low can you go? Where does it end? Maybe you compromise on the things that aren't as important to you, like height, or where the person lives. Then, the things that don't affect you as much, like bad blood in the family. You can compromise on everything, and what you end up doing is basically talking yourself out of everything you really want in a relationship. At the end of it all, you have no one to blame but yourself: in your head, you negotiated the worst possible deal for yourself. It's not this new boyfriend's fault that you didn't maintain those boundaries.

If you're new to dating, it helps to make a list of traits that are really important to you in a mate. That can be whether they're divorced, how they feel about their job—everything. Get down to the nitty gritty. You want a partner who talks dirty while you're having sex? Put it on the list. You want a partner who likes to dance? Put it on the list. This isn't a way to limit yourself. It's not a list of product features! The list will give you some guard rails while you're dating. You will be able to see where you're compromising immediately.

We are so susceptible to love. I get it. You want the romance, you want to feel special, and that makes it easy to get pulled toward somebody who's really not suitable—and isn't who you're looking for, either. It can be tempting to throw caution to the winds and say, "I'm open for love, no matter who gives it to me!" But that doesn't make you a free spirit. It sets you up for disappointment. Using a list and staying accountable to it can keep you out of trouble.

Dr. Gluck: To some degree, people adapt to one another. You can negotiate with your partner, for example, to do the dishes after dinner, and give something back. It has to be a give and take. You can divide tasks like planning family vacations or getting the car serviced. But, as we said, the essential elements of their personality are probably not going to change. With that in mind, let go of the idea that "love conquers all." Love and support from a caring, committed partner will get you through many challenges.

Love will *not* change who your partner is. Even if that person adores you and wants to make you happy, they may not be able to change themselves to suit you.

This is why it's important to come to dating with clear eyes and clear expectations. Your dating journey should always focus on finding out who the other person is. Learning what they're like. Spending time together. Lasting love comes when you build a relationship with someone who satisfies you and allows you to form an emotional attachment to them. It doesn't work as well when you get involved with someone based solely on mutual attraction, and then try to mold them to your ideals.

Rori: We have all these romantic stories about how love changed people or opened their eyes. It's sweet, but so unrealistic. How many times have I heard a woman who's just exhausted by her relationship? She's been banging her head against the wall for years, waiting for her man to grow up, act differently in some way, or give her what she wants. I want to say, "Honey, you should've known he was like that when you got into it with him!" It's a waste of time to keep hoping your partner is going to change. You can save yourself the heartache by selecting someone who already checks your boxes.

I want to point out that the people who believe that "love conquers all" really do believe that. It's romantic. They might feel that deliberately picking a partner by looking at their traits first, and letting the attraction come second, isn't natural. To each their own—I'm not trying to change anybody's mind! I can say, those people either end up getting lucky in their selection of partner *or* they float from relationship to relationship. They're driven by the

169

attraction, and because the people they pick aren't a fit, they end up having to move on. I get it, feelings are powerful, but you've got to take care of yourself, too. You can't just assume that because you've got a crush on the hot delivery guy or whatever, that he's your soulmate.

Dr. Gluck: He might be.

Rori: Yes, sure, he might be. But you wouldn't know that until *after* you've gotten to know him. A crush is a feeling, an instinct. It might be chemistry. It isn't a sign from God that he is the one with whom you're meant to be. So often, I see people who are accomplished, polished, professional, and successful in every way just go head over heels over every little crush. They don't know how to handle it. They're so convinced by their emotions that "this is The One" that they forget all about what they bring to the table and what they need and deserve in a relationship. It's like they're *eager* to sell themselves short in the name of what they think is love.

Never settle, because you will regret it later. Love in such a way that makes you feel free. The person with whom you're meant to be is a support to you in your life. You want an equal partner. To go back to the business model comparison, you don't take just any person on the street and make them the VP of a company. You vet them. You make sure they can actually invest. Not everyone can play at your level, so instead of lowering yourself to be more accessible, have high standards. That's how you end up with a platinum pairing: two power players, equally invested, with clear expectations for the relationship.

If you do get rejected, try to think of it as a good thing. You didn't get what you wanted in the moment.

Something better will come along. Keep in mind, "rejection is God's protection." If that one date didn't work out, or you chose to walk away after a couple months, that's okay. It's not a reflection on you: it simply means it wasn't meant to be.

Is There Any Such Thing As a "Perfect Ten"?

Rori: Yes. But my "ten" might be your "eight."

Dr. Gluck: It's a matter of taste. Everyone's needs and desires are different.

Rori: I think we can all agree on a few things, though. Right? When you're setting out to date, you're working on yourself, getting ready to find your match. We all share some values and beliefs about what's attractive. Maybe someone else's idea of what makes a handsome face is different than mine, but we can both agree that we want a good-looking partner.

Dr. Gluck: Absolutely. Physical health, fitness, a healthy mind, and good grooming are the bare minimum for personal attraction. We covered these basics in Chapter One, when we discussed how to maximize your chemistry and attract a potential mate. Natural selection favors individuals who are at their peak: young, sexually appealing, wealthy, and well-known. As we get older, our priorities change. Sure, some traits may still turn your head. However, I don't think it's "settling" to pick a partner who is age-appropriate for you. Again, relationships are extremely personal choices, based on your individual values. One must also consider that people age. As they age, their looks should be replaced by all the experiences that you have together and the depth of relationship that you have. People fall in love later in life, too. Things will change. You have to be able to realize that things will change and be able to accept this. As you get older, love goes from the eyes to the heart.

Rori: You're instantly attracted to what a person looks like, how they smell, and how they look. That's how it is. Lasting relationships are based on the things that last, though. I wouldn't describe a woman in her fifties, who's raised two or three kids, and founded her own billion-dollar dynasty as "older." She's not a damsel in distress. She's experienced and wise. She takes care of herself and knows what she likes. She's sexy, without compromise. That woman is a "ten."

Same with a guy who's in his early thirties, ambitious, and starting to get traction at the firm where he works. He may not have as much to offer financially as a more established man, but he's got potential and drive. He's not the youngest, and he's not the oldest, either. If he takes good care of his body and has learned how to be respectful, he is a "ten" also.

Defining your date with a number is kind of arbitrary, but it works! If you go on a date with someone and you come home tingling, so happy, and you can't wait to see them again—that's a "ten."

Dr. Gluck: If you find yourself dating several people in a row who are okay, but don't give you that zazazou feeling, you're hanging around in the "eight" zone. They're perfectly nice people. It may be fun to spend time with them. They may only be able to offer half of what is on your wish list. Until you find someone who genuinely makes you happy, do not settle. Your "ten" is out there. It would be sad to miss out on your "ten" because you wanted this whole dating thing to end.

If you've tried dating someone and it's just not working out—your values are different, or your schedules just don't match—you can walk away with grace. Pick up the phone and call them, or arrange to meet for a conversation. If it's not a fit, don't try to force it. You don't need to explain every little thing that you think they're lacking. This isn't about their shortcomings. It's about your needs, and what you consider a perfect match to be. So, be kind. You do owe them the courtesy of saying that you don't want to continue. You should know them well enough at this point to know how to go about doing that, without being hurtful.

Ghosting someone, or vanishing after a period of dating, is cruel to do, especially when emotions are beginning to form. This is more common in internet dating, where people treat one another like they're disposable. We do it differently: with class and grace. If the person was worth your time when it seemed like they might be a match, they're worth your time to have the other conversation, too. Saying "no, thanks" to someone who is essentially a good person but not *your* person is hard. But it's the right thing to do, and it will allow you to move forward without hard feelings or hang-ups that you carry into the next partnership.

Rori: Dating can feel like an endurance sport sometimes. I get it. Trying over and over again can be really exhausting. Don't settle for a "six" because you're tired or discouraged. In that case, it's better to take a break and just love yourself for a while. Always check your motives for wanting to couple up with someone. Is it because they are a "ten" or is it because you want a date for the holiday party? Are you settling because all your friends are married and you feel left out?

Your "ten" is based on *you*, not other people. This really is all about you! Your timing, your needs, your desires. You know that you can't rush quality. What works for you should work in every way. You're worth the wait—and the person you love will honor that and know that they're incredibly lucky to be with you. They'll see you as a "ten" as well. When you meet someone who's at the top of their game, and they understand and respect your worth, you're beginning to create a platinum pairing.

Is it a match made in heaven? No. It's a match that can take Manhattan.

Chapter 10

When "You" Plus "Me" Equals "Us"

As romance blossoms into a lasting relationship, you'll find that your attitude about your partner evolves. You'll go from "dating" to "dating seriously" to "committed." That's the magic of love: two separate people become one couple. Emotions and shared experiences create a powerful bond that can feel unbreakable.

For some people, this transition from "you and me" to "us" happens fairly early on. Others need more time to develop this connection.

One of the most important transitions any relationship goes through is this sense of deep commitment. This emotional bond can't be rushed—and shouldn't be, either. Relationships are created moment by moment, day by day. When you're falling in love with someone new, you experience a series of "firsts." Your first kiss and your first fight are equally important. They both tell you about who you're choosing to be with, and what kind of pair you'll become.

What happens when two people turn into a couple? They both change in subtle and significant ways. This chapter includes intimacy-building activities that will help partners navigate coupledom. Rori and Dr. Gluck's combined half-century of experience with happy marriages helps inform this intimate chapter.

175

The Next Stage of Dating

Dr. Gluck: About four months after your first date, when you've gone out for a while, you're entering the next stage of dating. You've found someone who is a "ten" in your eyes. Then, things become serious. Since this is the commitment stage, that means no more outside dating. If you've kept things quiet, it means no more secrecy. You can be "Facebook official." Family and friends should know about the relationship. You can talk about exciting adventures that lie ahead and sharing a future together. The pace of your relationship means that this stage can arrive sooner or later, depending on your ages and how well you know each other. But the younger your age, the longer you should wait. When you are older, you are more mature and faster to dismiss the bullshit.

In this stage of dating, you've spent enough time together to know how the other person looks in the morning. You have glimpsed different sides of the person and learned that there's more to them than the person you met on your first date. If you've included family gatherings and community, you have met each other's family eccentrics by now. Even normal families have the crazy uncle or the reclusive cousin. You're starting to share your worlds with each other and create a space in your lives that is all your own.

Rori: At this point, if everything is going well, you should want to make a commitment to be exclusive with each other. It's the right time, the right person. As a woman, you don't want to demand commitment. That's not sexy. You want the man to take charge: it's better if he's the one stating that he wants to be exclusive. In one of my earlier relationships, I dated this one guy for a *long* time. He wouldn't commit and kept saying he didn't want to get married. So I broke off the relationship. I wanted to get married; he didn't. I was ready to move forward, and I was not going to drag him through it, kicking and screaming. I did not give him an ultimatum. He knew how important marriage was to me.

As soon as we broke up, of course I immediately attracted interest from other men. *They* were willing to step up to the plate. My ex saw this and tracked me down. He proposed on the spot.

The moment when commitment enters your relationship is not the time to take it easy or be on your best behavior. This stage is the ultimate test of what your relationship can handle. It's the time to be your most genuine self. You have to be painfully honest about what pisses you off and what turns you on. If you don't talk about it now, it may not come up until after the wedding—and right before the divorce. Let the other person know what they're getting into. And you need to know what you're signing up for, if you keep this commitment!

My idea of life is to maximize pleasure, minimize pain. Let bullshit be fertilizer, not dinner. Since honesty begins first in the mirror, I suggest you take a look at yourself in a mirror, and say, "Is this person worthy of me?" If the answer is yes, even when your guard is down, that's a sign that you've found yourself a keeper.

Dr. Gluck: This stage is when your relationship climbs toward greater commitments and, ultimately, marriage. It's when you explore everything that you would never consider discussing before now, for fear of putting a damper on things. But this fire needs to be tested. So pour all the water you want on it. If it's real, the fire won't go out.

By now, you should have proven that you can do a weekend trip with this person and get along. You'll be settling into the day-by-day routine of a relationship. You have concerns about what life will be like with this person in the future. That's fine, but don't think about *decades* at this point. Five years can be your benchmark. This depends on your age and the progression you see in the relationship. Farther than that is not worth thinking about because no one knows what's going to happen.

To continue building trust, you must be even kinder and more respectful to your partner. If they're showing you all these important, intimate things about themselves, you need to honor that. Maybe a tenth of people take liberties at this stage, certain they can get away with something. They go back to flirting, or panic and start looking for a little relationship on the side. They may suddenly become emotionally unavailable because they are afraid of what it is all leading up to. But this stage should be the exact opposite. The greater the commitment, the greater the priority with which you should treat the other person.

We talk about the genuine self. But who is that person? The genuine self is the real you. Your genuine self is formed by the individual journey you've lived, philosophies you've acquired and integrated into your life, original thoughts, attitudes, beliefs, education; all of which may or may not agree with your family and/or culture. It's the journey each person takes to examine themselves and figure out what they believe. There has to be a genuine *you* before there can be a genuine *us*.

The genuine self is also defined as the person you want to become: the person with whom you are ideologically comfortable. You make a commitment to try to express and live that. For people who aren't living their genuine self, they have to take time to actualize that self. The sooner they do that, the sooner they will be at peace— and the sooner they will be in a place where a relationship has a chance to be successful.

In this next stage of dating, you commit to your partner by living your most genuine self with them. It's another layer of you. This sharing should deepen your attraction to each other.

Rori: Let's talk about what happens once there's a ring. It changes everything! Commitment, to me, means there's jewelry involved, on top of everything else. That can really complicate things. I believe that the engagement can be the worst time in the relationship. It's no longer you and me, now it's you, me and *them*. Everyone has an opinion. You might wish you'd just kept it a secret! The shorter the engagement, the better off the couple will be. It leaves less time for bullshit.

Dr. Gluck: Engagement rings have two historical meanings. First, it was meant to be a built-in dowry. The ring was the dowry the man gave the woman to purchase her from her father. The size of the ring had to do with the wealth of the family. The second meaning was that it's the way to pre-seal the marriage contract. Under law, even Old English law, if the man broke an engagement, the woman kept the ring. That's still the rule. If the man breaks it off, she keeps it. If she breaks it off, she gives it back.

If Rori was breaking up with a man, even if it was a fifteen-carat Tiffany diamond, she'd give that back.

Rori: Fifteen carats is what am I worth, baby! The perfect relationship is my guy, my diamond, and me. I'm partially kidding, of course. I love rings, but I love my guy more. I always say, I'd rather have my dinner at McDonald's with my soulmate than at the Four Seasons with some asshole.

That jewelry that a man gives you can be a big help down the road. The second I got my divorce I took all the jewelry my first husband gave me and took care of myself. I had to get a car, find a new place to live, and pay my own way. Those jewels were my security.

Dr. Gluck: I don't believe in the ring. The first time I got married, we didn't have any money for one. I was twenty or twenty-one, working three jobs, and still two years away from finishing my PhD. At our wedding, I was so poor that I borrowed money to buy a wedding ring. I borrowed a suit, and even my shoes. I took my wife home to an empty apartment with a mattress on the floor. But we loved each other, and that's what we wanted to do.

Rori: But that's where you were *then*. It's romantic! Now, you're more established, so you would give your wife a ring.

Dr. Gluck: If that's what she wanted, yes.

Rori: I'm saying, if you don't do the research to get to know me and know my taste in engagement rings before you propose, you don't deserve me.

Dr. Gluck: We agree that you shouldn't make a decision for another person. If you're making a decision for another person, they should have greater input. The woman wears this ring for life. It's her hand, her look. So you should take her to the jeweler.

The price of the ring should be in proportion to what the couple wants their lifestyle to be. It's not necessarily equal to three month's salary, or anything like that. If the man knows the ring is important but a down payment on a new house is more important, he can say to his prospective wife, "This is the budget for your ring. Having a home together is more important, so in three or four years, I can replace your ring with a bigger one."

They need to have a conversation about how they want to make their future together.

Rori: Every girl dreams of her ring. Wrong ring, wrong guy.

Dr. Gluck: With the ring, it should be a man's celebration of his wife's identity. She should be involved in picking it. Does he have to kneel down? Absolutely not! He should start his relationship by being exactly who he is. The biggest problems in relationships are when one partner says, "That isn't what you were like in the first three months, when I met you, and now you're like *this other person!*"

Maybe it's going to be great and maybe she'll dump you, but at least it's real.

Rori: Always keep it real!

Dr. Gluck: Is the ring worth living for three years in a place that's not going to make you that happy? The ring becomes either less or more significant. If the woman leaves, the ring goes anyway. The question is, what's going to make us happier? How young or old are you? If you are already established, the ring will be bigger. If you're starting out, you need to decide if a ring is more important than living in a nicer neighborhood, sending your children to a better school, and mixing with better people.

The ring is a small symbol in the bigger picture of the relationship. Then there's the wedding.

Rori: Everyone waits for their wedding. It's so exciting, but it brings out the worst in people. If you can get through the engagement, you can get through marriage. Family, friends, and money get involved at this stage. It's not you and your significant other alone in your perfect little world anymore, but all these outside influences. This can really test and potentially ruin a relationship. You have to stay on the same page and really trust each other. Otherwise, you risk being torn apart because you weren't able to communicate. If you really want to know if you're meant to be, plan a wedding together. Talk about family drama! Everything comes into play, from your bank account to who's going to sit with your weird uncle. Lots of couples can't do this: they break up, which may be for the best.

Commitment to each other is the most important thing here. You put your significant other first, even in family disagreements. For example, a good friend of mine was engaged to a successful CEO who came from a great family. His mother was speaking to my friend about her other child—the groom's sister—who was *also* a successful CEO. My friend's mother-in-law had the gall to say to Patty, "I don't want you to get jealous of my daughter. She makes more than enough money and they are a double-income family."

Fortunately, my friend's fiancé stood up for her. He told his mother that she was out of line. If he hadn't done this, the marriage could have gotten off to a very rocky start. He had to pick between taking his mother's side, or his bride's. He did the right thing and it helped them avoid future issues with the family.

Falling in Love Without Losing Your Balance

Rori: Love is one of my favorite things. I'm obviously in the right business. I get to create matches and help people discover their platinum partner every day. It means so much to me to see those relationships grow, and all the good things that come with it. The right partner will make you rich in love—and in other ways, too. Love creates children, a home, family, and everything worth having in life. No wonder I love love!

Dr. Gluck: Love is an adventure. It's life's greatest experience. It changes people in ways that didn't seem possible. When you put two people together, and they fall in love, you start to see what they're innermost qualities. The person who seemed stubborn is actually very loyal and honest. The person who had many insecurities, was actually frustrated about being alone. Relationships don't fix us: they show us ourselves. You can think of marriage as a mirror. Your spouse is the person who's closest to you. They see you at your best and celebrate your successes with you. And they also witness you at your worst: at the end of a long day, in a fight, when you're both out of patience. They see your vulnerability. They see your genuine self.

Make no mistake about it. Relationships, like love, are always evolving. The moment you take for granted what you love, is the day your love is dismantled.

Missing out on love because you're afraid to fully share yourself with another human being is a loss. It's a loss to you and a loss to the world. Luckily, by building that foundation of trust with your partner—through dating, spending time together, and getting acquainted—you can create intimacy. That intimacy makes anything possible. Through intimacy, people are able to be honest with each other. They can talk about difficult topics. They are able to work together to make a life worth sharing with one another. This sounds simple, but it is actually a long, intricate process: a dance between two people.

We emphasize that traditional, even "old-fashioned" approach to dating because it gives you time to see what your date is like as a partner. Committing too quickly or trying to hurry to get to the point in the relationship where you feel safe, sacrifices those small moments that are important opportunities for building intimacy.

Now, those moments can be sweet: holding hands, slow-dancing, singing to one another. They can also be moments of conflict. You will have times when you can't stand the other person. Even early on, you might bicker. This is how you learn about each other. Whether you're sharing a kiss or a little fight, you're experiencing what it's really like to be with each other. That's authentic connection, and that's why we fall in love. Never cause unnecessary pain, when it can be avoided.

Rori: The temptation, in dating, is to just dive in and forget about everything else. Job? Who cares, you call in late. Kids? Get a babysitter and spend every night with your sweetheart. Family? They can take care of themselves, you're in love! Now, that's the kind of reasoning that not only destroys healthy bonds in a couple, but also wrecks your sense of self. That's how high school kids do relationships. They glom onto each other and become a single unit. They spend every second together and nothing else matters. Romantic? I guess, if you're a teenager. We are adults, so that playbook is not going to work.

There is no point in being in a relationship that makes you feel like you're not yourself anymore. It can be so nice to snuggle up to someone, settle into that role of the "boyfriend," and let everything else go by the wayside. When you do that, you let go of your agency—the special qualities you have that make you independent. You give up all the little chances to have that playfulness with your partner. The back-and-forth fun quickly becomes flat and uninspired. Just like you might throw a pinch of jealousy into the mix to spice things up, you want to hold onto your individuality. If you're agreeing with your partner on every little thing, you will lose the tension that keeps your chemistry bubbling. If you want to get engaged with a ring, stay engaged emotionally.

Dr. Gluck: When I was younger, and even today, people want to seem cool to their dates. Cool, detached, calm, easygoing, down for anything. I can tell you that those who are *too cool* can find it hard to find lasting commitments. Why? It's like trying to nail Jell-O to the wall. There are no rough edges. Well, that might be

185

appealing, but there's also nothing on which to hold. Where's the intimacy? Where's the spark? It doesn't last, because the person who's too cool is just going to slide right out of your life.

Total passivity is rare in human beings. We all have strongly held opinions about something. Those big feelings may not come out every day, but they're there, deep inside us. Every person has interesting stories, ideas, and moods. If Mister Cool is like Jell-O, the opposite is more like Mister Velcro. He's got *texture*. He's got hooks and rough spots and it's much easier to connect with him. He may not be perfectly smooth, but he's got good material with which to work. A partner's imperfections are not necessarily "bad" or undesirable. They're the mechanism that allows you to create intimacy. The person who's afraid to show their emotions, or voice their opinions, is going to undermine their relationships because there's nothing with which to connect.

Rori: I would say I have a strong sense of self. My personality is always front and center, even when I'm on my best behavior. I'm very polished, but you know I keep it real. You never have to guess what I'm thinking—I'll tell you! Now, for some people, that reads as "extra." Like, too much. I don't agree. I live authentically. People know what they're going to get with me. It actually encourages connections because people are drawn to that. They see me as someone who knows her own mind and isn't shy to speak up. People respond positively to that quality. It gives them permission to speak up, too. So, instead of preventing me from forming meaningful relationships, my personality actually attracts others.

Dr. Gluck: For people who are insecure about finding a long-term relationship, that's the temptation. They think they need to dumb it down or to exaggerate and make yourself seem more important than you are in order to be more appealing. In reality, you just need to be yourself. The relationship where you're faking it, or holding back, is not one that you're going to keep. If you ever feel, in dating, that you're not able to be yourself—move on. That is a sign that the other person is not a fit.

Getting lost in your partner is another unrealistic expectation for romance. If you ever feel like you're being swept up, and it's causing you to lose sight of who you are, take a breath. Your values should guide you—not your desire to be partnered. It's fine to go slow. Just because someone sweeps you off your feet doesn't mean you should totally lose your balance. A good relationship reinforces your sense of individuality, instead of erasing it. Here are a few questions to help you check in with yourself as your relationship develops:

> Can I be myself when I'm with my date?

> Do I like the way I talk and act with them, or am I less than my best self?

> When was the last time we did what *I* wanted to do? When was the last time we did what *they* wanted to do?

> In my ideal relationship, conflict is _____.

Lead with Your Frontal Lobe

Rori: One of my rules is to date for a year. See the person through all the seasons. The test of time is the best test for your commitment. It gives you time to answer the big questions: *Where's this going? Are we going to live together? Become engaged? Get married?*

It's a bad idea to skip a stage. No matter what your emotions are telling you, stick to your guns and make sure you aren't getting lost in the excitement of being in love. You can't build on a relationship that lacks an emotional connection, but, at the same time, you can't let that emotional connection make all your decisions for you.

Feelings aren't facts. When you fall in love with the wrong person, it's like forbidden fruit. The relationship is thrilling but you know it isn't right for you. That's when your reasoning brain has to enter the picture. Your emotions might make you feel addicted to this forbidden fruit. There's nothing like forbidden fruit. It always tastes the sweetest. You love his or her personality, the way you feel when you're together. When that happens, your rationality is out the door. Your logical brain is out to lunch. You feel like you are not in control. You do things and know it isn't who you are.

Commitment to the wrong person rocks your world—not in a good way. You know it's not good for you. The hardest part of committing to the wrong relationship is when you truly know the person is toxic, but you can't do anything about it. That's when the rational brain has to step in and kick your ass a little.

Dr. Gluck: The emotional brain—the animal brain—makes quick decisions. It is very good at being in denial and will sweep stuff under the table that gets in the way of what it thinks it wants. The emotional brain is a conglomerate of all of the people and things that have influenced you to this point. It is subjective, not objective. Its attachment to a significant other can be addictive. The emotional brain wants what it wants. The heart also wants what it wants. Then, five months later, the frontal lobe knows what it knows, and the relationship is over. There is a caveat here. People in love use less than one percent of their frontal lobe. Most people are rational with everything else: life, goals, career. When it comes to love, it's all about emotions. That frontal lobe is stuffed in a closet and is just screaming to chime in.

Rori: And you've just spent five months on the wrong person, who you probably knew was wrong for you all along. You just didn't want to see it. The pitfalls we talked about in Chapter Eight are real. They don't just break your heart: they waste your time. They bring you disappointment and they may even ruin your belief in love. The frontal lobe isn't trying to ruin the party. It's trying to protect you from getting hurt.

Dr. Gluck: This rational part of the brain, which is more connected to individual identity, clarifies what is going to create long term happiness for you. That's where your values live. Your rational brain can veto or confirm whether or not you're going to progress in a relationship.

So, you have to ask yourself, "Which would I rather have: stability and calm, or heights of great passion, sorrow, and joy?" Believe it or not, it's different for everyone. Each of us has a level of risk we're willing to take. Our tolerance for uncertainty in relationships is often a result of childhood experiences. We have to know ourselves well enough to understand what our level of risk is and how to work with it or move beyond it.

Neurologically, the animal brain is about survival. Your logical brain helps to create something sustainable. It's concerned with what is *good*, *better*, and *best*. The rational brain will keep a relationship going for a long time. But without the emotional brain, you'll feel that something vital is missing. If the opposite is true, you'll have a series of very exciting, short relationships that feel meaningful but are impossible to sustain. That's why, in any stage of a relationship, it's important to keep your priorities, needs, and desires in mind. Be alert for red flags, whatever those might be for you. Enjoy the journey, be present in the moment. And listen to your brain as much as you do to your heart.

Rori: Being infatuated will only take you so far. Your brain can only handle those intense feelings of being in love for a certain amount of time. That romantic, swoony feeling is good. It helps to propel your relationship along. People with great naiveté and lack of experience get damaged when the "in" love part is replaced with love and respect as well as peace.

In the commitment stage, your brain has got to kick in and start answering the hard questions. Assuming you'll always feel butterflies when your boyfriend calls is about as smart as assuming the S&P NASDAQ will go up every day. That's not reality. There are ups and downs. Eventually, the relationship moves into a combination of love and respect. You love the person, and you know *why* you love them. You understand rationally why you're attracted to them.

Dr. Gluck: Don't rush to get a ring on your finger, or you'll end up with a band-aid there instead. Even if you're older or feel like time is a factor, let the dating process spread out over time. Don't see the person too often. Sprinkle in your friends. Continue to watch for red flags. The stages of dating hinge upon a number of factors, and commitment is no exception. The younger people are, the greater their tendency to get involved quickly, to fall in love fast. Intense attraction doesn't mean the love is healthy or long lasting: both people are still changing.

Rori: Love means you have a feeling you can't live without the other person. If you've been around at all, you know that love on its own is not a guarantee of anything. Pay attention to what your instincts tell you. Is jealousy still a problem, even when you're formally engaged? Is your sweetheart suddenly not so sweet and his love is in question when it's time to plan the wedding? Do your friends all say the same thing about the person to whom you're committed—and it's not too good?

Let your rational brain do its job in this stage of dating. Your heart should still be speaking loud and clear. Your brain can tell you things that your emotions can't. If someone is really down on their luck and you're still there, that's love.

Commitment starts from chemistry, but there's so much more in between the "Nice to meet you!" and the "I do!" You have to get to know the person before you can love him. When you commit to someone, go through a crisis with them, and come out as a couple to your friends and families, it provides insight into the person's character. There's no such thing as unconditional love. Deep love starts in the heart, but it's minted and printed in the mind.

Chapter 11

My Sugar's Sweet When You Stir It Up

Both men and women should define what they want from any relationship. Some relationships, like those between sugar babies and sugar daddies, have a more transparent arrangement than others. Unfortunately, these types of relationships often carry negative connotations. Some people view them as wrong or even immoral. But that morality is measured in a completely subjective way. The relationship shouldn't be denigrated just because a person is using money to attain something of value to them. The relationship is as legitimate as any other, as long as both individuals are being fulfilled by something they value.

If you're a wealthy woman and you want someone much younger than you, and you don't mind if the relationship has an expiration date, then go for it. Everyone enters into relationships with their own unique expectations.

This chapter discusses unorthodox "arrangements" between couples and why they work. Couples who seek a more traditional relationship can learn from these arrangements, and improve their love lives as well. Rori and Dr. Gluck will talk about how sex, money, and love are intertwined.

Window Shopping for Weekend Fun

Rori: We're all adults here. We don't call names. To really engage in the art of relationships, we need to destroy the myths about certain words. Men and women who date multiple people should never be degraded. Yet, they're commonly referred to as whores, players, sluts, and other derogatory terms. It's gross. What someone else chooses to do is nobody's business but their own.

Dr. Gluck: People who are sexually adventurous are actually wise to gain experience, to explore their options. It took my wife and me less time to fall in love than it took us to find the right house in Connecticut. We saw hundreds of them. In the same sense, why would you want to commit to someone when you haven't fully explored what's out there? And, within the relationship you're forming, why commit before you've gotten to know everything about each other?

Even though young women in some cultures get married at nineteen or younger, I have yet to see a wonderful relationship develop when one or both partners marry in their teens. If they ever enjoyed fantastic sex, or even stimulating conversation, it quickly falls off.

In Western culture, parents should rethink the idea that a daughter should remain a virgin until she is married. What happens is that she'll marry the first man who kisses her.

Rori: People have been shopping for love for a long time. We just call it by different names. Online dating is one way of arranging your own marriage. Other people trust a matchmaker to find partners for them, or their families put couples together according to their traditions.

Arranged marriages have existed for thousands of years. Marrying for love is new in comparison. Which one works better? I think it depends on a person's unique expectations. Falling in love doesn't necessarily lead to staying in love. An arranged marriage can develop into a loving one. At the other extreme, it can be a lifelong cold relationship, a marriage of convenience. The big difference between an arrangement and a love-match is that when you marry for love, it's only the two of you calling the shots. That's empowering. However, it also means that you might lean too heavily on romance to compensate for some of the weaker elements in your relationship.

I will tell you that love is great, but anything that creates an imbalance in the relationship will chip away at that special connection. One characteristic that sets arrangements apart from a love-match is that love isn't the primary reason for coming together as a couple. In an arrangement, with romantic love off the table, other factors will influence whether the relationship is a keeper or not.

Dr. Gluck: In these scenarios, *everyone* has an agenda. Both parties are providing what they want and need. The younger person is providing what the older person wants, which is agreeable to the younger person. This can include anything from companionship, to the status of being with a younger person, to financial security. What does the younger person get out of the deal? It might be a luxurious lifestyle, protection for the future, or a unique itch that both partners want to scratch. Sometimes—but not always—sex is part of the arrangement.

The understanding between the couple is that the relationship has an expiration date—which is usually when the older man dies. It's not intended to last past the time the terms are still agreeable to both parties. Yet, aside from the benefits that each partner receives, many of the elements of the arrangement is not so different from ordinary dating. My advice to individuals looking for sugar daddies and mommies is to first know yourself. That is really where everything in dating starts and ends.

Rori: Very often in this type of arrangement, there's a need for an objective or second eye. You need the advice of other people to make sure you're getting into it for the right reasons. Are you compromising yourself because you love seeing the deposit hit your bank account? Do your girlfriends call bullshit when you gush about your sugar daddy?

Dr. Gluck: In your new arrangement, just like with regular dating, be clear about what you are offering and what you are expecting. Talk about how long you're interested in sticking around. If you can be honest, the connection will last. Once you know what you're working with, it will be much easier to identify the type of person you are looking for. Is your sugar mama much older? Sugar baby, much younger? This isn't a marriage, so the age difference can be considered more objectively. The same thing is true about your financial arrangement and how welcome your partner is in the other parts of your life.

I'll tell you right now, if you're a gold digger— someone digging for money just to enjoy a luxe lifestyle— the arrangement will be *very* short-lived. You haven't fully read the prenup. If you have no real interest or curiosity about the other person, then expect to be treated in the same way. But if you can come to it with clear expectations, without compromising your values, you can expect to get that back, too.

Get Your Hands Off My Bottom Line

Rori: If you're a woman looking for a sugar daddy, you probably don't care if the man is twenty, thirty, or even forty years older than you. You have an agenda. You know what you want. You are actively looking for someone who is going to take care of your expensive tastes and you're willing to give something he wants in return: sex, companionship, nurturing.

Every case is different, but as we said, there shouldn't be any negative connotation. Those people who judge another person's choices are usually unhappy with their own choices and with themselves.

Take a woman who is divorced, has emotionally and physically healthy children, and is looking for a partner. She's entrepreneurially engaged in running a business that is not as successful as it could be. She might choose to find a sugar daddy, who could act as an angel investor in her company. Or how about a young, beautiful college student who is going to be over a hundred and fifty grand in debt before she graduates? She's gorgeous and knows what she wants. She isn't averse to finding a sugar daddy who might help her cut her school debt in half or eliminate it altogether when she graduates.

Dr. Gluck: We see a similar dynamic in ordinary relationships too. A number of men and women prefer younger partners. It isn't just an economic deal, but an attraction that can include mentoring and a deep connection to a family member who has made an impact in their lives. The older partner can bring a wealth of knowledge and life experience into the relationship, which enriches it. However, in my experience, the younger person has an exaggerated sense of what they really bring to the table. Nowhere is it written that youth automatically means better sex, conversation, or more empathy.

Rori: In a normal relationship, the woman's agenda is not to find a man specifically to say, "Hi, I will go out with you if you pay for my children, my lifestyle, and my expensive tastes." A woman who's simply attracted to older guys isn't a gold digger in the sense we're talking about. If a man falls in love with this woman, he would take on the responsibility of her children as part of their relationship, right? That's not an arrangement at all. They would build a home and family together. People's traditions and cultural beliefs play a huge role in how their relationships develop, and how much "arranging" actually happens prior to a formal commitment.

You have to ask yourself: What do you bring to the table? Do you have your own value? Do you have a personality?

Dr. Gluck: Another important question is, do you allow a man to develop for himself and explore and not get on a his case? What men love is their freedom. If someone can give them immense freedom plus not punish them when they come home, that's worth a tremendous amount. Listen, men are just as shallow as women. And catty! If a woman doesn't look a certain way, she's not worth their time.

Rori: You have to know yourself, in any kind of relationship. If there's certain things you want, make sure you're willing to pay the price. If you're signing up for the trophy, you will pay the price to get it. You also have to think farther down the road. If you are a young, beautiful woman who starts a sugar baby relationship at thirty-three, and you stay in that arrangement for six years, you're now thirty-nine. You might want to have a marriage and a partnership, but your arrangement hasn't prepared you for that. Will you be able to have children with your future husband? It's probably too late. Also, some very good men will not be interested in you as an equal partner if you've been a sugar baby. They'll pass; they won't be able to see you as a wife because you've been in that lifestyle for so long.

If you make that choice, know that it affects your future. What happens if you want to fall in love and start a family? Will you be prepared, or fail because all of your relationship skills are related to finance, not romance?

Dr. G: If you're really shallow, you will drown in deep waters.

Rori: There are consequences. Not everyone cares about them, and not everyone even gives it a second thought until they suddenly experience regret from missing out on something meaningful. Arrangements are fine, but is your sugar daddy keeping you a secret? Is he saying he'll leave his wife for you? A man with money and power can have the world at his fingertips, and even if he's taking care of you, you can also be taken advantage of. You have to be careful.

Dr. Gluck: A man doesn't have to be a millionaire to have an arrangement. What happens if the potential sugar daddy is a man who is making a relatively low salary for where he is living? What kind of woman would be a possibility for an arrangement? One option is traveling to a less developed country. A man will go to a third world country where his normal salary translates into a fortune.

The woman he finds in this third world country is grateful to the man. Her fear of fulfilling her basic survival needs is alleviated. She has hit the jackpot. The man has found someone who will love him for the rest of his life because he has changed her status. No one is looking at him as an older man or judging him for partnering with a younger woman. When it comes to survival, all the rules change. Note: Don't take a trip to New York City anytime soon with your new wife. Once she speaks English, you're dead.

Rori: I was twenty-six years old when I met Charles. I already had a child. I came from a wealthy family, so it wasn't as if I was looking for an older man who had money. But I am attracted to older men naturally. I like the dynamic of a relationship with an older man. I feel the need to respect, admire, and learn from the person who is going to be my partner. That doesn't negate my power as a woman. I can certainly be submissive in the areas where my partner has more wisdom and experience.

Dr. Gluck: Yet, so many of the elements are similar to a formal arrangement. It never ceases to amaze me how people project their reality on what they see, rather than taking the time to get to know the situation which they find so easy to judge.

Rori: One thing that I wish more young women would be aware of in their relationships—whether they're arrangements or not—is that learning from your partner is so important. Don't just let your man catch all of your fish for you. Have them teach you how to fish. Gain experiential knowledge from them and let them mentor you in areas where you can grow. No matter what happens, you can always take this experience into your future. It's something that money can't buy.

Dr. Gluck: We have a client in her forties who likes being a sugar mommy. She's attractive, makes good money, and when she got divorced, discovered that she loved her freedom. She likes being in control. She *can* be in control. She definitely doesn't need a man for his money. However, she is realizing that integrating a bartender or a starving artist into her world is difficult. It's nice to be able to go to an event together. She doesn't want to have to hide her partner in a closet.

In real life, the first question people ask is, "What do you do?" If you're a philosopher or a professor, great. You have an intellectual gift that the average millionaire doesn't have. On the other hand, the millionaire has something the philosopher doesn't: money! It's fine if you don't have a pile of cash and you and your partner are comfortable with that. If there is balance in the relationship, then it can work.

Rori: In a healthy relationship, one thread can't be expected to hold everything together successfully. Arrangements can rest entirely on a simple transaction: companionship for cash. A relationship must have many different threads.

If you are from an affluent family and partner with someone from a different level of wealth, you have to be very careful. You need to be sure of the other person's agenda and motivation for being with you. Do they want me for who I am? Do they want me for the lifestyle I can provide? Do they want me for the newfound status they would gain? If a successful man loses his fortune, is there still love?

If you truly believe you are in love and both of you are on the same page, then you can make an adjustment to live in a different manner than you've known previously. One-sided arrangements, where one partner is taking advantage of another, are the worst. They never last, and at least one person walks away much worse off than when they started the affair.

Dr. Gluck: Take, for example, a wealthy woman who chooses to be with a man of lesser means. She can afford to take care of him, but is that what she wants to do? Does *he* want that? Even though you can't control with whom you fall in love, you need to be sure your ideals and goals match. If you're the woman in this scenario, be sure your boyfriend is not a taker and is in the relationship for the right reasons. Money masks a couple's problems. There truly can be an expiration date, even in a regular relationship. There's a world of difference between a "sometimes" love and a "forever" commitment.

Money may be just one aspect of a relationship but it is more than just paper. It represents security, freedom, and the ability to make choices. With money, you can choose any restaurant you'd like. You can go wherever you want on vacation or buy any piece of real estate that suits you. There is a huge difference on how you view money as a young student compared to how you view it when you enter the real world. Once you gain experience, you come to realize money represents freedom and choice.

Having said all of that, a great percentage of the world lives in poverty. There is a richness to the relationships—that is not monetary—in these couples' families, that is more valuable than many wealthy families bank accounts. In less developed countries, family spend more time together as a whole. You see close bonds between spouses, children, and extended families. Time spent with extended family is a gift. Money can't buy that.

Rori: What's shameful, though, is that a person with money is more respected than someone without as much. Is the definition of a "good" family one that has more money? No, of course not. But that is often the misguided perception. There has to be a balance.

If You Want Some Sugar in Your Bowl

Dr. Gluck: To clear up a misconception, sugar relationships between men and women don't always include sex. Sometimes it all boils down to companionship, a person with whom you can be yourself or enjoy events and obligations. And yes, for some people there are bragging rights as well.

Arrangements that don't include sex are more common than you might think. Older men who have severe diabetes and can't achieve an erection might be a sugar daddy. Then there are men who have erectile dysfunction and want a no-pressure partner who is understanding and responsive. (I'll say that 95 percent of the time, ED is psychological. There are many forms of treatment.) It is a myth that removing sex from a relationship will destroy it. Many relationships have a foundation of great sexual relations and they end up in flames, and there are phenomenal relationships that thrive without sex.

Rori: Oh yeah? What relationships are those?

I get that there's a difference between closeness and actual sex. There are ways of touching someone without sex. You can kiss, hug, find other ways of feeling intimate. Being with a partner who's healthy, that should be fine. I understand that our bodies change over time, and there are obviously situations where you want to be understanding, not demanding. But turning away from your partner for no reason, denying them physical intimacy, is not alright. One partner in a relationship can't call all the shots on every sex decision—or every money decision.

For me, I know that my love language is physical touch. I can't be in a relationship without touch. God forbid, you're in a situation where your partner isn't well, or there's an accident—I would not ever leave the person because they can't perform in bed. I wouldn't want them to leave me because I couldn't have sex, either.

Sex should never be used as a weapon, like, "I'm not going to give it to you because you're an asshole." A normal, healthy, sexual person who's not getting it from their partner will find it somewhere else. Once you're doing that, you have really destroyed your relationship.

Dr. Gluck: Breaking from tradition, like the kiss good morning and the kiss goodnight, should also not be used as a weapon. Ignoring your partner or the silent treatment should not be used as a weapon.

Rori: Swapping sex for security is something you do in sugar arrangements. It's a trade. That's something that shouldn't happen in non-sugar relationships.

Dr. Gluck: Sex isn't everything in sugaring. They may have sex with their sugar mama, but they will find a lover elsewhere. The older person needs to be understanding of that. There's love-making and there's sex. You can have sex when it's not possible to make love. The guy who can't touch his wife for the nine months of her pregnancy has basically screwed himself. He needs to be on her like white on rice.

When you absolutely can't share physical intimacy, partners can substitute emotional intimacy and shared goals. This is less common in arrangements.

If there is no explicit arrangement, in what you are engaged is a de facto relationship. In these relationships, partners should never turn to each other and accuse them of entering into the partnership just for sex or money. It is imperative in every relationship that both partners express their intentions from the start. Conflict is natural, disappointment is inevitable, but anger and distrust are deal breakers.

Within my private practice in New York City, the melting pot of the world, I treat a significant number of CEOs and billionaires. One client told me he knows his partner is in it for the money, but he doesn't care. She gives him everything he wants, treats him like gold, and he can show her off. When he wants sex, she is more than willing.

Some women, for whatever psychological reason, can't see themselves with someone their own age. They prefer older men. Then there are men who never grew up and need a younger woman, and sometimes a woman wants a man twenty years older. There are also women who want a man twenty years younger, but their expectations of faithfulness are much less realistic than that of a man's.

Rori: I say, it's not the years, it's the mileage. I like a man who's seasoned! Age doesn't matter to me but experience definitely does. If I was dating a man my age, I would feel like I was running around with a puppy. I like that my partner is polished, sophisticated, and well-traveled. That's hot. The qualities to which I am attracted seem to come with age.

Because I prefer older men, from a cultural point of view and the way I grew up. I don't want to be with a man who's a babysitter or doing my errands. My father was a man's man: he was a protector and a provider. My mother stayed home and took care of the children until we were older and settled. Then, she started her own business. These are the values with which I was raised. I don't want Mister Mom. I also don't want a man who works from home. Get out, go to work! Everyone has their role to play.

Dr. Gluck: In this world we live in, women should always be treated equally in terms of their access to education. They should be paid on par with a man, and they should be treated with respect. However, when a woman enters into the relationship with a guy, if she's smart, she will realize that you have too many hundreds of thousands of years of baked-in cultural messages that say the woman is the nurturer who creates a home and the man provides financial support. For many couples, one salary doesn't do it, so strictly traditional roles are not realistic. The man, in that relationship, needs to find another way to enjoy his partner.

Stereotypes are there for a reason. There are men who are more nurturing and can be a better primary parent. There are women who are more nurturing as well; if they are, they have the better qualities for childcare. *Co-parenting* is essential.

Rori: Real talk, everyone needs to have their desires fulfilled from a relationship. I don't care if you're a sugar daddy or a sugar mommy or a sugar baby. If you're happy, who am I to judge if that's what works for you?

Dr. Gluck: If you're a sugar baby, mommy, or daddy, you're a member of a rather unusual club. Is your arrangement meeting your expectations? Are things working out as you had hoped? Let's take a deeper look. You can do this activity alone and never share it with a soul in the world. Or you can fill out your respective sections and compare notes.

For sugar babies, are any of these statements true?

➢ I entered into this arrangement out of desperation.

➢ I entered into this arrangement out of curiosity.

➢ My arrangement works for me.

➢ This arrangement is fair.

➢ What I like about my arrangement is:

_____

➤ What I dislike about my arrangement is:

       _____

For sugar daddies or sugar mommies, are any of these statements true?

➤ My arrangement works for me.

➤ My needs and desires are being met for what I signed up. I feel fulfilled.

➤ I feel great affection for the other person.

➤ I treat this relationship and the other person honestly.

➤ What I like about my arrangement is:

       _____

➤ What I dislike about my arrangement is:

       _____

Bear in mind that people in non-arrangement relationships can ask themselves these questions, too. Are you happy with what you are receiving out of the relationship? Does your relationship feel like it's based on love, or on an exchange?

How About Money, Honey?

Rori: Without money, love is hard to sustain. That might not sound very romantic, but it's true. Your relationship needs a solid bottom line. Money can't buy happiness, but it puts a hell of a deposit on it. It mitigates the problems that can lead to a breakup. In a modern relationship, love comes first. In an arrangement, it's all about finances and value. Who's giving what, to whom, and why? Love doesn't keep receipts, but your sugar mommy sure does.

If you were married at twenty-five and divorced at forty-five and are now getting back into the dating world, romance is going to feel unfamiliar to you. You might have been in a relationship that started to feel more transactional or businesslike, rather than loving. It can be hard to get back into the mindset of being open to romantic love.

For example, I received a call from a woman in her forties who has been divorced twice. She was in a rather fragile state. She was just getting back into the dating world. That Friday, one of our clients expressed a desire to meet her. By Sunday, when she called me, she still hadn't heard from him. She was nervous and upset. The guy was very wealthy, and she thought he might be the one to pay for her Park Avenue apartment. She was used to being in the lifestyle where a man would care for her: she had bills to pay!

I explained that I didn't know what her date might or might not do. If he cancelled for some reason, I told her, "So what? Nothing has been lost."

She kept saying, "It's been two days, is he going to cancel? Would he do that?"

She didn't know how to relax. To her, every date was high stakes: she wanted the immediate validation of an arrangement, not the pleasure and anticipation of a relationship. She had demands, not expectations. Those are hard to meet in a relationship that is new and undefined. For her, this date was a transaction. Love was not coming first. What she really loved was the lifestyle to which she was accustomed.

This is the trade-off about which I'm talking: the man is getting a trophy and the woman is getting the security. She's trading sex or emotional labor for security. A man often chooses a younger woman for this kind of arrangement because he thinks a younger partners will have more energy to put into his family, especially if he already has children.

Dr. Gluck: In the example Rori shared, the lifestyle to which this woman was accustomed was more important than the sense of wholeness she could have in a normal relationship, on a day-to-day basis. Background and culture are significant details for people whom place money before love in a relationship. They may be from a family or community where money is a status symbol. There are exceptions. If you happen to come from an intellectual family where everyone is a professor, then your status will come from your job as a department head at MIT. Or if you're a rabbinical scholar, you don't make much money, but you have greater status than a brain surgeon within your community. There is still prestige, but it is linked to something other than your paycheck.

Part of the reason people place money (or status) above love is that love is perceived as a fleeting emotion, completely dependent on factors that change constantly. But every couple has a final deal-breaker. It's usually financial or tied to stability in some way. Once that line is crossed, there's no going back. For one person, it may be that the partner is leaving bills unpaid. There may be calls from collection agencies. It could be bankruptcy. For someone else, it may be the family's housing situation.

For example, a patient of mine had five children and a husband. They were all living in a tiny apartment so small she couldn't raise her children properly. She felt like she couldn't breathe. The relationship with her husband ended because her expectations for their home life were not met.

With a man and his sugar mommy, there tend to be fewer disagreements, less friction. They have defined roles. When you partner with an equal, the relationship can start to feel territorial. If both people are alpha-types, two strong people, it can be really difficult. Each person is going to have specific strengths. When love comes first, you can honor what you each bring to the table without making it about the receipts.

Dr. Gluck: The Platinum Poire method is designed so that people don't have unrealistic expectations. In the same way, you shouldn't have unrealistic expectations. We touched earlier on keeping an open mind about whom your next partner can be. *Requiring* very specific attributes—physical or otherwise—is something that happens in arrangements, not in relationships. There's a difference between a personal preference and a requirement. That preference is fine for you to have, but don't make it gospel.

For example, if you're looking for someone in a specific age group, you may have problems. Let's say you're a woman who is fifty and you want to date a man who is not a day over forty. If age is your *criteria*, not your *preference*, you might be happier looking for a short-term arrangement rather than a younger husband. There are times when this does work out: that's the exception, not the rule.

211

Rori: We bring value to the relationship in so many ways, though. It's not just your age—age is just a number! When evaluating a client, I have to be visual. What does the woman look like? Is she physically fit? What type of energy does she radiate? What's her personality like? If she tells me she wants a man who makes two hundred million dollars a year, what is she bringing to the partnership? Some men don't care what the woman does for a living. She could be a yoga teacher making twenty-five thousand dollars a year. But she has to bring value. It's not just about looks, either. Haven't you heard? "No matter how good she looks, somebody somewhere is tired of her shit."

Dr. Gluck: An arrangement is easier to find than a soulmate. People know that, and I think it keeps them from seeking the love of their dreams. The friction there, is between what you want and choosing to settle for what's easy.

We humans have an insatiable need to connect. Loneliness is such a profound, painful, and empty emotion. When people settle for the easy way out of loneliness, it doesn't turn into love. It turns into conflict. You might be tempted to replay the song from the seventies: *if you can't be with the one you love, love the one you're with.* Deal with the pain, swallow it, and make sure you have some good friends to get you through. Sugar may be sweet, but it gives you a cavity.

Rori: Whatever it is you need, you can find it. It's about what you're willing to do to get it, and what you offer in exchange. A genuine connection, based in love, is very different from a business proposal that develops into mutual

212

affection. If you're a person who needs romance, don't mess around with sugaring—and vice versa. You deserve to be happy and have your needs met, on your terms.

Mastering the art of relationships isn't about trying to fit a square peg in a round hole. It's not trying to make something fit that does not fit. It's finding the match that fits effortlessly and with ease. If you let the match speak for itself, then there is no struggle in the process. You'll know right away, in your gut, what you need. A weekend treat, or a lifetime love? Evaluate your desires and your personality and do what's right for *you*.

Dr. Gluck: Why do arranged relationships outlast emotional ones? You can't commit suicide jumping out of a basement, that's why. The high expectations of a romantic relationship are asking you to jump from the hundredth floor. The fall is what gets you. In a low-stakes or no-stakes arrangement, there's no risk—and not much of a reward.

Rori: That "reward" keeps people in the lifestyle, though. They find it hard to leave because it's easy, convenient, and has a certain amount of cache. If this kind of arrangement is what you want, fine. But before you sign up, think about how sugaring will affect your future. Is this something you want because you have a short-term goal, or are you going to be a kept woman (or guy) for life? A two or three-week arrangement is one thing. Three years? No way. Just like you'd assess an ordinary relationship, think about where sugaring will lead you—not where it can take you.

Chapter 12

Power Couple Problems

What is a power couple? They're two people who are attractive individually and magnetic when they're together. They're charismatic. They shake things up. Power couples draw the eye: they are *the* influencers in financial, political, social, communal, and even spiritual ways. Although there are plenty of well-known power couples in the news, power couples exist in every part of society. Whether they meet at a park or at a charitable event, when they couple up, it's electrifying.

Belonging to a power couple can be a mixed blessing if you're not ready for it. Power couples don't just stand apart from other pairs. They also need to follow different guidelines to keep their connection healthy, mutually beneficial, and balanced. It takes a healthy relationship to hold two big personalities together.

From fashion to philanthropy, power couples make their shared passion work on a broad scale. How do they do it? What draws them together? In this chapter, Dr. Gluck and Rori will examine archetypal and iconic couples and talk about the dynamics when two powerful people come together.

The Power of the Platinum Pair

Rori: *Poire* is French for "pair." We focus on couples, matches, and dynasties that are built to last. The platinum pair is the ultimate, desirable relationship. It's what happens when a pair of people are brought together for a mutually shared purpose. They have that sexy energy. They have passion. They can do great things together, or separately. Who wouldn't want that?

Dr. Gluck: With a power couple, you're not dealing with two individuals. You're merging two powerful entities into one. The stakes are higher. The egos might be bigger. The emotional needs are so different. As two people come together into a relationship of this caliber, there's a period of negotiation. More than anything, power couples understand that commitment isn't to be taken lightly. Their relationship has a public component: they know they're being watched, sometimes maybe even envied, by their community, the people around them, and possibly the world.

That means that people entering this kind of relationship, or who desire to be part of a power couple, need to be extra sensitive to one another. There has to be a philosophical alignment, goal setting, and skills for delegating. If any element of the relationship isn't sufficient to withstand the incredible pressure of being a couple in the public eye, it will crumble.

Rori: Yes, and then you've got a huge mess on your hands. When power couples break up, it's a cultural moment. Think about Jeff and MacKenzie Bezos, or Angelina Jolie and Brad Pitt. (Or even Jennifer Aniston and Brad Pitt!) Those breakups give people pause. Every little aspect of the relationship is dissected, judged, and picked apart. The gossip is real. If several million people *all* have an opinion about your marriage, that is probably enough to make you take it seriously!

Dr. Gluck: But the same guidelines for those couples apply to people who are big fish in their respective communities. It doesn't matter whether one hundred people are watching you, or one hundred million. Power couples know that the way they behave has significance.

Power couples should go through the stages of dating more deliberately than other couples for two reasons. First, there is more pressure on them in the press, so they should really take it slow. Successful couples who are loved in their community have the same issues as the royal family. They may not cope with the international paparazzi, but they'll face the same level of scrutiny in their own town. The second reason to take their time is personality assessment. Just because two people are rich, famous, and admired doesn't mean they have anything in common. It's better to date discreetly and ensure you're totally compatible before making a relationship public.

When you have wide influence, you have a responsibility to the people whom are around you. Power couples need to be mindful of this when they get together.

Rori: The personalities are bigger, and that means the problems can be bigger too. Each person is used to getting exactly what they want. They're used to being the star, but relationships don't work that way. You can't have one person coming in second. Compromise becomes more difficult when you have two strong personalities in the same room, and they're both accustomed to hearing "yes" all the time. Something's got to give.

In a power couple, both people bring significant value to the table. That doesn't necessarily mean financial worth. It can mean beauty, sex appeal, social influence, or special skills as well. When there's an imbalance, or one partner fails to acknowledge the contributions of the other, there's going to be an issue. Typically, the man is the one who has more money. The woman is beautiful and accomplished but has less financial clout.

It's different when the woman is the one with the money. Then, the man's ego comes into play. Let's say a couple in their thirties get together. She's a partner in a law firm and he's a social worker. She is making a million bucks a year. He's making thirty-five thousand dollars. He's a wonderful man. They're a very attractive, socially modern couple. They agree he's going to stay home and raise the babies while she works and is the breadwinner. Five years later, they're divorced because she comes home from work one day and asks him, "What do you really do?"

But if the situation is reversed, and he's the big lawyer while she's home with the kids, that's less of a problem. That kind of relationship is perceived as fine. Double standard! The underlying issue is still about money, because the person who is the primary earner has more power in the dynamic.

Dr. Gluck: It's important for people who are dating to evaluate their power dynamic early in the relationship. This may eliminate competition between you and your partner and help manage expectations. When you're dating, think ahead of what you can or can't accept.

➤ What are your strengths?

➤ What are your partner's strengths? What do you value about them?

➤ Do you and your partner have special attributes, values, or skills that you reserve only for one another?

➤ How do your partner's strengths complement yours, and vice versa? Do you work well together, or are is it better to work separately?

➤ Do you feel completely comfortable if your partner takes care of you financially?

➤ If your partner earns more, does that make you feel like you're worth less?

Rori: Look beyond the love. Examine the realities of daily life and what your deal breakers could be. It's better to have no relationship than a relationship that erodes your worth and values. Do you really need someone in your life who doesn't pull their weight? Balance and equality become even more important when you're together at the top.

Sometimes, the biggest deal-breakers in power couples come from unexpected conflicts. For example, if you answer every single phone call you get when you're with your girlfriend, that might show her that she's a less important part of your life than your agent or your business partners. Saving some part of your life for "just us" is extra important. That closeness must be protected.

Dr. Gluck: In power relationships, there can be an assumption that each member of the couple is somehow "better than" other people. That's not the case. They're not set apart by some inherent virtue or value. In some ways, they're worse off. Wealthy, famous people often have problems that are even harder to solve than the every-day person faces. Fame is isolating. A famous person's emotional issues can be amplified. Being half of a power couple doesn't mean that someone's early childhood is resolved. They're beautiful and rich, but they're struggling even harder, especially when their upbringing was rooted in rewards and not being taught responsiblity. That's why you should never envy anyone.

Authenticity is one of the biggest hurdles to forming a power couple. It's easy to date a "fan," or someone who's eager to be in a support role. But is that in the relationship's best interest? If a person is infatuated with who they think you are, it's not going to work. Power couples have to work extra hard to be intimate with one another, away from the demands of public life.

If you can handle this type of high maintenance relationship, the rewards are worth it. Power couples build up one another. For example, if two department heads are a couple, their academic orientation gives them a step up. Together they have credibility and influence in a meaningful way in their field. A businessman and an artist may be a power couple as well, because they have shared influence. They really do also empower each other to be the best versions of themselves. They're trendsetters.

Rori: What happens in your relationship has to stay there. You have to be extra discreet. All the people who love to keep up on what you're doing, also love to see you fall! The more private you can keep your romantic business, the better. Once it's public, it belongs to everyone. Gossip can really hurt power couples. Don't fight about the headlines, what someone else is saying, or how you're being perceived from the outside. Don't argue with each other about what's actually happening between the two of you: *communicate*. Bleach your dirty laundry before you take it to the street.

Dr. Gluck: In every couple, but *especially* in a power couple, you have to show a united front. You have to work as a team, even when things behind the scenes are rocky. Whether you teach at a university or manage a Fortune 500 company, the rules for power couples don't change. The next sections will each talk about iconic power couples and how they balance their public image and their private lives.

The Power of Pop Culture: Kim Kardashian and Kanye West

Kim and Kanye are unquestionably the most influential media couple on the planet. *The New York Times* referred to their marriage as "a historic blizzard of celebrity." Kim became known as a celebrity in 2007 when she first appeared on reality TV. Since then, her notoriety has grown. She models, started her own cosmetics line, and is a best-selling author. People say she's "famous for being famous," and that might be true. She's one of the most powerful influencers in social media, with one hundred and thirty million Instagram followers. Every word she says, every public appearance, and every outfit she wears is newsworthy.

In 2015, Kim was named one of *Time*'s "One Hundred Most Influential People." That year, she made over fifty-three million dollars, and was 2015's highest-paid reality television personality. *Vogue* described her in 2016 as a "pop culture phenomenon."

Kim's marriage to rapper Kanye West is her third. She and Kanye have three children together.

Kanye is a more mysterious figure than Kim. He's cryptic. Yet, everything he does—especially when he's with his wife—is scrutinized. He has over twenty-nine million Twitter followers and an avid fan following who love his music. His relationship with fame is long and complex. He started as a producer in the early 2000s at Roc-a-Fella Music, with Jay-Z. His solo albums have a cult following. Even through some mental health difficulties and drama with other stars, he's considered one of the best rappers alive. He also has his own clothing line and collaborates with other brands. He ties with Bob Dylan for having topped the annual Pazz & Jop critic poll the most number of times ever, with four number one albums each. He's won twenty-one Grammy awards, is one of the most critically acclaimed musicians of the twenty-first century and has sold over one hundred and twenty million records worldwide— making him one of the best-selling music artists of all time.

With a couple like this, drama and criticism are part of the daily routine. With every move under a social media microscope, it's important for them to be extra kind to each other and gracious when they speak about each other publicly.

Kim told *Elle* magazine that her marriage is strong because of their shared love for their children. She said, "I think it's important that in all couples, the mom gives the husband as much attention as the kids. [Kanye has] taught me to have more of an opinion. I've taught him to be a bit more calm or cautious. We're a good balance."

Rori: The relationship started while Kim and Kanye were friends. They are two peas in a pod. She gives a purpose to him: he was always in love with her, and he wanted her. She's his muse. From a creative standpoint, they're making money, building an empire, and raising children together. They have an incredible work ethic together.

Dr. Gluck: Very often, a couple is connected because of children. Kids leave home, pets die. There have to be many more personal connections to maintain the closeness. Clearly, shared love is great, but you must continue to grow beyond your children.

The Power of Philanthropy: Bill and Melinda Gates

What do you do when you're one of the richest couples in the world? Give it away, of course. Bill and Melinda Gates, who are collectively worth more than ninety billion dollars, are known for their joint generosity. They give millions away every year to philanthropic causes like vaccine research, water access projects, and other efforts to improve life on the planet for as many people as possible.

Bill Gates has been on the *Forbes* list of the world's wealthiest people since 1987. As a leader in the computer revolution, he founded Microsoft and is considered a pioneer in that space. In 2006, he transitioned to part-time work at Microsoft to full-time work at the Bill & Melinda Gates Foundation, which was established in 2000. The foundation was identified by the Funds for NGOs company in as the world's wealthiest charitable foundation, with assets reportedly valued at more than $34.6 billion in 2013.

Bill and Melinda have been married since 1994. Melinda has said that outsiders often assume that Bill calls the shots, since he was the head of Microsoft for so long and accustomed to making executive decisions, while she was at home with the children. However, in real life, that's not the case. In a 2018 letter to investors, Melinda wrote that true partnership and shared values helped them stay strong as a couple: "When I tell a story about what I've seen, [Bill] feels it. He might ask me to gather some data for good measure, but he doesn't doubt the reality of my experiences or the soundness of my judgment."

She also wrote, "It's always been important to us that we are equal partners in our foundation's work. We've learned over time to give each other feedback at home about times in the office when we didn't meet that goal. And we're better for it."

The Gates' relationship began when they met at work. Melinda was hired at Microsoft in the late 1980s and met Bill, the CEO, four months after she'd started. Since then, they've stayed united through partnership and philanthropy by sharing a common cause.

Rori: A man is the head and the woman is the neck. The woman can turn the head any direction she wants. His success rests on hers, and her success supports his. They both work for the same cause but they each have their own role to play.

Dr. Gluck: Bill is so confident in who he is. They both have a very strong individual identity. When you love yourself and have confidence in yourself, it's much easier to be a partner to someone else.

The Power of Sex Appeal: Alex Rodriguez and Jennifer Lopez

These two are hot, hot, hot. Jennifer Lopez is an internationally beloved singer, performer, and actress. She's in her prime and known for her independence. Because she enjoys such extraordinary fame and success, she does not need a man for his money or security. She also doesn't need a relationship for procreation: it's clearly about recreation. She has twins from her marriage to pop singer Marc Anthony, one of the three husbands she's divorced.

She's been in several high-profile relationships with men like Sean Combs and Ben Affleck. She's also "dated down," choosing partners like Casper "Beau" Smart, an unknown backup dancer who was eighteen years her junior. In relationships with less-powerful men like Beau, Jennifer kept a low profile but never lowered her expectations. She appeared to be happy to have a boy toy for a couple of years following her divorce: her relationship with Beau ended when there were rumors of him cheating. That was the end of it. Jennifer could clearly handle a serious imbalance of wealth, talent, and fame—but not disrespect from her guy.

Sex appeal is a big part of Jennifer's image. The infamous green Versace dress she wore to the Grammys in

2000 caused Google to create their image search option. *Variety* commented on Jennifer's appeal, saying, "She established herself as an oft-provocative sex symbol while her demeanor made it abundantly clear that she's not asking you to come hither."

Her current fiancé, Alex Rodriguez, is also incredibly sexy. A shortstop and third baseman, he's signed two of the most lucrative sports contracts in history. He played twenty-two seasons in Major League Baseball (MLB) for the Seattle Mariners, Texas Rangers, and New York Yankees. Rodriguez began his professional career as one of the sport's most highly touted prospects and is considered one of the greatest baseball players of all time. He is the record holder for grand slams, with twenty-five in his career.

The two were drawn to each other right away but kept their courtship traditional. Jennifer knew about Alex's reputation as a player; he also has two daughters from a former marriage. Over their first year, their public appearances became more romantic, including a trip to Paris. When Jennifer received her Video Vanguard Award at the VMAs in 2018, she acknowledged Alex, saying, "You're my twin soul, we're like mirror images of each other. My life is sweeter and better with you in it because you make me realize that every day the sky is not the limit, the universe is infinite and so is what we can accomplish together with love and trust and understanding. There is so much more to do, to experience and there's no one I'd rather do it with, baby. You're my macho and I love you."

Rori: Jennifer is Latina, and so is Alex. For her, because she's so rooted in her culture, it's an important value to share. It's clearly a bonus in her relationship. With someone who's age appropriate, who is a dad to children close to the age of hers, it's going to be easier. She's obviously with someone who brings out the best in her and vice versa.

The Power of Style: David and Victoria Beckham

David Beckham started dating the woman America knows as Posh Spice in 1997. David is considered one of the greatest soccer midfielders of all time. He played for Manchester United, Preston North End, Real Madrid, Milan, LA Galaxy, Paris Saint-Germain and the England national team, for which he held the appearance record for an outfield player until 2016. He is the first English player to win league titles in four countries: England, Spain, the United States, and France. He retired in May 2013 after a twenty-year career, during which he won nineteen major trophies. He also looks great without his shirt!

Victoria Adams came into the public eye as one of the Spice Girls, an internationally loved pop group of the nineties. She started modeling after leaving the group and has posed for fashion magazines and on the catwalk. She's considered a style icon: every one of her looks is captured (and critiqued!) in the tabloids. Like her husband, she's naturally associated with glamour, high fashion, and luxury. She launched her own very successful fashion line, starting with sunglasses and denim. They are highly sought after as spokespeople and ambassadors for luxury brands. They have four children: their two older sons have been recognized as style icons as well.

Through their long marriage—they tied the knot in 1999—the Beckhams have had to deny many rumors about imminent divorce, cheating, and other marital problems. They say the secret to sticking together is to be together, even when life makes it hard. Victoria says that David is her soulmate, and they stick together even when the noise gets to be too much. She told *Elle UK*, "David and I both respect that each of us are very, very busy; we are both running big businesses, but we do put the phones down, and sometimes we just talk."

David commented to BBC Radio 4, "People have talked about, you know, 'Do we stay together because it's a brand?' Of course not. We stay together because we love each other; we stay together because we have four amazing children, and do you go through tough times? Of course, you go through tough times. It's part of relationships, it's part of marriages, it's part of having children, it's part of having responsibilities."

Dr. Gluck: It's important to recognize that there's a significant price to pay as a power couple if you're both running your own businesses. Having five or ten-minute chit-chats is not a substitute for real, sustained time together. People in power couples tend to be workaholics, and that's one of the reasons they tend to file for divorce. With that kind of power, money, and influence, it's important to make *real* time for *real* relationships. You can't just build a business, you have to build the love, too.

The way a power couple is measured is not only in their influence on culture, but their influence on their offspring and what *they* become.

The Power of Creativity: Jada Pinkett Smith and Will Smith

Jada Pinkett and Will Smith have one of the most talked-about marriages in Hollywood. They've always been open about the importance of communication and trust in their relationship. Jada told *HuffPost Live*, "I've always told Will, 'You can do whatever you want as long as you can look at yourself in the mirror and be OK. At the end of the day, Will is his own man. I'm here as his partner, but he is his own man. He has to decide who he wants to be and that's not for me to do for him. Or vice versa."

Will Smith is one of America's best-loved actors. He has been nominated for five Golden Globe Awards and two Academy Awards and has won four Grammy Awards. He is the only actor to have eight consecutive films gross over one hundred million dollars at the domestic box office, eleven consecutive films gross over one hundred and fifty million dollars internationally, and eight consecutive films in which he starred, open at the number one spot in the domestic box office tally.

Jada Pinkett is his second wife; they married in 1997. Jada has starred in over twenty feature films and also performs in a metal band as well as producing films, documentaries, and TV series. The Smith family includes Jada and Smith's two children, as well as Will's son from his first marriage. The family is extremely creative, and support each other in dance, performance, music, and other media.

After more than twenty years of marriage, Jada and Will have made it clear that communication and trust are key to maintaining their relationship. Will said, "If there is a secret, I would say it is that we never [intentionally worked] on our relationship. We only ever worked on ourselves individually—and then presented ourselves to one another better than we were previously."

Rori: Every couple has the right to create their own rules. If it works for them, who am I to judge? You have to find out what works for you.

Dr. Gluck: Open relationships are heaven to some and hell for others.

Platinum Love Is Priceless

Dr. Gluck: Your relationship needs to be your priority when you're in a power couple. Have faith that the business, work, and success will still be there if you put your phone down for a few minutes and give your partner your undivided attention.

Rori: Your ideal partner will support your success, but they're not your assistant. Or your employee! A power couple has that balance of respect because both of the people in it are doing their own thing. They have their own lives. They enrich themselves independently, and you know what? That means they'll always have something interesting to talk about at behind closed doors at day's end.

Dr. Gluck: The 'power' in 'power couple' isn't just about social clout. It's love. The love you share as a couple makes you powerful. People look up to you, notice you, and try to copy what you're doing. You inspire one another, and you inspire the people around you. That's how your relationship can be influential and create positive change. To do that, you've got to find someone who can play at

230

your level, has their own hustle going, and is used to being the center of attention. When you find a partner who clicks with you, it can elevate your relationship—and you'll acquire plenty of good things on the ride up.

Rori: They say, "your ego is not your amigo." You may be a star in the outside world, with people hanging on your every word, but that doesn't mean you get to throw your weight around at home. You have to check yourself and be just as humble as anybody else.

It's one thing to be "Madonna" when you're at work and out in the world. At home, you're a wife. You're a partner. You're a mother. You leave your persona at the door.

Power Couples in "Mixed" Marriages

Rori: Being a power couple doesn't mean you have to agree on everything. Having a common goal or cause can be the reason the bond between you is so strong. However, differences of opinion are natural. You have to be careful that those differences don't create problems that can tear you apart.

Dr. Gluck: Love *can* conquer all things, even in marriages where the couple doesn't agree on life's big issues. Love wins, as long as there's a shared philosophy and principles.

Rori: I don't agree at all. Let's say you've got a couple where the husband is much more conservative, and the wife is a liberal bohemian type. Dating is fun, they live together, and they're talking about the future. He may not mind her super easy-going nature, but does he see her raising their kids? Differences of opinion about politics,

231

ideologies, and religion have huge repercussions for a couple's potential. If you can't agree, you can't really commit.

Dr. Gluck: No, I believe love and respect can overcome ideological differences. There is a caveat: love is not a noun, it's a verb. It needs to be put into action and proven over time.

Rori: But in a couple where one person is to the right and the other is to the left, you can't pretend like you won't fight about that stuff. You have to define your goals. Otherwise, you lose your power and you end up tearing each other down. Marriage is hard enough. It is much harder when you come from two totally different religions, or political affiliations, or cultural backgrounds. If you're having children, it makes things even more challenging.

Dr. Gluck: In that case, I think a mixed marriage would be beneficial. You could both respectfully show your opinions and raise your children to have an open mind. You would help the kids see that there's more than one perspective and way of being in the world. The kids can make their minds up for themselves.

Rori: Not in my house! I grew up in a modern Orthodox family. I'm used to raising my children in a different household. My kids went to private school. Intermarriage is a big, big no-no in my community. I could never imagine being married to a man who's not Jewish as well. It's important to pass that on to your children: it's part of their heritage, and part of your legacy. When you're raising kids, you have to have a united front. You don't want to confuse them. You want to give them something strong from which to build. My husband Charles always says, "A family divided is a family defeated"

Dr. Gluck: I was married to my first wife for twenty-four years, until her death from breast cancer. She was Italian and Catholic. Every week, I took our kids to a different religious service. We visited many places and participated in many traditions: Buddhist, Baptist, Adventist, you name it. I would explain the history, the values, the application of these faiths. They took everything in. It helped them grow and have that open perspective. Today, they both have friends all over the world with different values. For myself, I would take spirituality and kindness over any organized religion.

Rori: But what's *your* religion?

Dr. Gluck: On paper, I'm a Stoic, but I would never join a religion that would accept me. My religion is the beliefs and values I have, which is more than some people can say. How many people from a religious home actually practice those values on a day-to-day basis? Avoiding gossip, giving to charity, turning the other cheek. People are more obsessed with their religion as an identity than actually following it. They say, "I am this" or "I am that." Exploring each other's faiths will broaden your horizons.

Rori: I don't think you can say that about politics, though. It's so charged these days. You can get dumped because you voted for a candidate the other person doesn't like, or because you believe in a cause that your partner thinks is bad.

Dr. Gluck: Respect is a spiritual principle. It's universal, even when it's not universally applied. In relationships where you come from different political

233

affiliations or you have different opinions about feminism, birth control, or gun control, you have to come to the table with respect. Some people don't recognize that when you conduct yourself with respect in the relationship, it makes you stronger. It keeps the focus on your shared values. People can coexist without agreeing.

 Rori: But some people don't believe in anything!

 Dr. Gluck: Belief in nothing is belief in something. You have interfaith couples, who come from different cultures. You have people who are spiritual but not religious and agnostic people. Atheism is a religion: it's just a very depressing one.

 Rori: I just think it's easier to stay within your culture. I'm thinking about the kids here. When raising children, it's 'monkey see, monkey do.' When you eliminate conflicts about spiritual beliefs or religious commitments, it simplifies things. You know what your comfort level is about your beliefs, so you need to decide if you really want to bring an outsider into your inner circle, and why. Attraction is one thing. If you're in a power couple, you need to look beyond your preference and think about your family and your community. You know yourself and your own family, so you need to think about it. Can you date someone from a different faith? Will your partner be accepted, or are you fighting an uphill battle and setting yourself up for failure?

 I want to make it clear that I'm not opposed to mixing. I just think you should go into it, knowing the challenges of diverse backgrounds. It's not something you take lightly. Even small differences can cause big conflict. For example, if one person is Ashkenazi and one is

Sephardic, it can be a problem. My father used to tease my mom because they were from different cultures. Even within a culture, there can be differences.

Dr. Gluck: Open communication keeps the power flowing within a couple. Once communication breaks down, the relationship is essentially over. Are your differences making it impossible to talk? Then, you've got a problem. You really see that now, in this political climate. The country is in a political fervor. Politics is a divisive subject. Philosophical differences are part of that, and it puts strain on couples who don't see eye-to-eye on certain things.

Rori: You think that's stressful. What about power couples where one or both of them are actually in politics? You think it's easy to date across party lines? There are so many things that would make that just impossible, unless it was exactly the right combination of people.

Dr. Gluck: The eternal question: can the elephant and the donkey really get along?

Rori: Only if that donkey doesn't act like a jackass! Look, you see high powered couples in politics all the time. The White House, for example, is always the home to America's first power couple: The President and the First Lady. All eyes are on them. They're talked about all the time. Sometimes, they're both politicians; other times, the First Lady takes a humanitarian role or acts like a support for her husband. But you know for sure that they don't argue about policy at the annual Press Corps Dinner.

Once you realize you and your partner don't agree on everything, you really have to keep things private. A power couple may have disputes, but they should *never* make it open to the public. There's a time and a place for political and religious discussion. However, you should always appear to be cooperating, having fun, and enjoying life together. Otherwise, people will talk.

Politics are important at home and in public, too. Would you bring someone home who's very conservative, when your family are all super liberal? You have to be respectful of your family, your partner, and yourself. Is your family going to flip out? Do you really want to put your partner through this? If you think it's not for you, don't do it.

Dr. Gluck: If your ideology is the most important thing for you, find someone who shares it. That's like any other value: if you can only date like-minded people or people of the same faith, then don't go out with people who don't match your preferences.

I feel that a couple can find common ground and respect in everyday life. Do you have to agree on everything? No. No couple does. It can work. Remember that politics is like fashion: it changes every season. Love, on the other hand, is eternal. Love is much harder to break, but anything neglected will eventually decay. The love you share is the most precious thing you'll have in this life.

Rori: That, and Harry Winston.

Dr. Gluck: Put your dignity before your diamonds, though!

Rori: Diamonds are the extra sparkle in a beautiful life. It doesn't have to be a bed of roses, but with the right person, even the simplest life feels like heaven, because you are together.

Dr. Gluck: I'm struggling to imagine you finding a home on the range.

Rori: Hey, I didn't come from filet mignon. If I love the guy, I could definitely do a hamburger.

ACKNOWLEDGMENTS

RORI:

To my other half. My husband, my love, and my mentor in life. You are the true definition of a life partner. Thank you for all your support in making "the art of dating" such a wonderful experience—and for showing me that when you have the right partner – anything is possible. To my children, Butchie & Helen, Grace, and Cesar—you inspire me to be the role model to show you that the sky is not the limit. To my step children—Dov and Aliza, Carolyn and Ronnie, Ariel and Deborah, Thank you for all your love and support. Dr G - The person who saw the potential in me and made the investment—am truly honored. Laurie—Thank you for spending countless hours on getting our book cover to be a true work of art. Jessie—Thank you for the months and months of editing, writing, and re-writing. For knowing my voice. You have proven to be completely invaluable. A BIG THANK YOU to Claire Rudy Foster for your guidance in having this book come to fruition! You made our dream a reality! Sabrina, you are more than a Publicist and Manager- you are a game changer, and a dear friend. Jill Tornopsky & Allen Antar, to my parents, thank you for your unconditional love and support. Especially my Mom who has been by my side every step of the way—you're a true rock star.

DR. G:

My wife Mirela, daughters Leanne and Melissa and
Socrates. There is not enough room to write how much of a
support they have been in all my endeavors. Rori has
blossomed into a force of nature. If there is something
above an "A type personality" Rori would be in that
category. She has been the fire behind the project. She
crosses every *t* and dots every *i*. I can't help but thank the
thousands of philosophers, writers, and historians. Each of
who have given me a part of their soul. Through their
words and writings I definitely would not be who I am
without them.

Made in the USA
Middletown, DE
23 March 2019